GW01605276

DIRECTORSHIP

DIRECTORSHIP

A. Person

FAUVES PUBLISHING

Published by Fauves Publishing

First Published in the United Kingdom in 2022

The paper used to print this publication and the manufacturing processes conform to the environmental regulations of the country of origin.

A CIP catalogue record for this book is available from the British Library

ISBN: 978-1-7396579-0-1

Designed and typeset by Tetragon, London, in Sabon MT Pro
Printed by TJ Books, Padstow, Cornwall
Project and Print Production by Booklabs Ltd, London, Booklabs.co.uk

Contents

Acknowledgements

There are many people I would like to thank for their help in writing this book, both directly and indirectly. What started out as a notebook filled with notes in 2018 has finally reached a point where I feel it's ready for printing. For that, I owe particular thanks to those who pushed me to take the work off the shelf in 2021 and rewrite it, and the friends and family who read early drafts with patience and good humour. Others have kindly pointed out areas of improvement or given encouragement and criticism for my thesis or sections they read. I would like to thank my family above all, for their patience and understanding of my obsessive focus. Thanks, of course, to my editor and all of those who have been involved in the design, printing, and distribution process. Your professionalism and care are deeply appreciated.

For those left unnamed for their own reasons, you know who you are. Thank you.

Introduction

The fundamental problems of politics and its philosophical underpinnings can only be solved by bringing about an end to politics as we know it and having it evolve to mean something new. Foundational questions defined by philosophers over two millennia ago still plague us and despite the apparent progress made since, politics and our sociopolitical systems have yet to truly evolve to maximise the benefits to humankind.

The gains of freedom, liberty, and rights that people have made since the French Revolution and the enactment of the American constitution are receding. These trends are accelerated by the technologies that could instead be used to increase our freedom. We stand at a sombre inflection point, but there is yet time for humanity to paint light on our collective canvas. Politics needs its 'Copernican moment'. Something as significant as that change when we shifted from believing the Earth stood at the centre of the universe to the understanding we have today of the solar system. The difference is that, unlike science, it cannot come from a single source, lab, or thinker, but rather must be built by us all, individually and together, for our mutual benefit. Enabled by existing technologies, in the same way that Galileo made use of the telescope to change science forever, the politics that we know today might become what alchemy and astrology are to chemistry and astronomy. Absurdities to be remembered as distant history and only truly understood in retrospect. In politics, that kind of progress may even simply be a matter of choice.

This book borrows ideas from the history and philosophy of science to focus a lens on our sociopolitical structures. Politics sits within a Kuhnian paradigm, which is defined by the nature of political representation. In short, we are represented, politically, by others. While this appears to be obvious or even mundane, this book argues that it is this facet of politics that defines and contextualises our political existence, group interaction, and the structure of our world. Shifting to a world of self-representation would move us into a new paradigm and definition for politics. We are stuck in a primordial political paradigm and this book seeks to explain why this is so and how we can move past it, imagining what it might be like to live in another, more equal, world. Arguing that by changing just one factor that hides in plain sight, we might yet change everything and allow politics to progress and evolve and come to mean something entirely different.

This book is also about moving beyond the concept of citizenship; that we may become something more: Directors. Truly equal and empowered, we could, in a new political paradigm of self-representation, all share in a part-time vocation as lawmakers; remunerated fairly for our service and enabled by existing technologies. This book then looks at concepts such as belief, law, culture, identity, self, collective, and equality, imagining what those words might come to mean if we take the chance to build a truly different, fairer world. We might come to see ourselves and humanity differently and, sharing a new high status, treat each other better and deepen the source of the rights we cherish that are increasingly being eroded in today's world.

Most of this book was written in 2018 and 2019 and then put aside for the first year of the COVID-19 pandemic. When returning to it in early 2021, I had to ask myself whether I felt my thoughts were still relevant in a world that had changed so much. I believe that they are even more relevant now than then. Initially conceived as a series of notes and a personal thought experiment, I did not write with a view to publishing until well after the first draft came into being. I wrote this for myself, to learn something and, displeased with the political belief systems out there, to find something that would give me peace. Much in this book is personal, despite it being public in the nature of the ideas addressed. Whether or not there is resonance remains to be seen. Perhaps it is too personal for people to identify with. Only you will know.

This work can also be thought of as a series of essays that follow a loose chronological order. These are neither academic nor, as creative experiments, 'plans of action' or a blueprint. They exist, rather, in the humble hope that little pieces might help someone, somewhere along their journey, or that of their group. A bit like lighting a match in the dark so others can find the light switch. If you read this book and find that you are not there with me, that's okay, I can sit here, in the dark, alone. Politically, we all do, even if we just don't know it yet. This book seeks to highlight that fact: true progress in politics has yet to come.

The reader will find that some of the essays are entitled 'Etudes'. This term, taken from the world of classical music, essentially defines studies around a certain topic. Mine are meant to be used as tools for further thought and research. Points of departure and creative experiments that are in no way meant to be stand-alone chapters or even concrete thought.

Why 'A. Person'? Why not a real name on the cover? There are two reasons. First, if this book doesn't resonate then my name doesn't matter. Second, if the work does mean something to you, then you will understand why it is that my name shouldn't matter and that I shouldn't become a representative of an idea. I am, after all, no more than one person among the eight billion alive today. Perhaps one might dare to dream that this book could become the beginning of a first draft of another book written by literally everyone, a political GitHub as it were. The other, more personal, reason I have not put my name on this book is that, although both Montesquieu and Corregio may have signed their works, I am a humbler painter.

The reader will find terms and words that are new or that I have invented. I have, at times, had trouble finding words for situations, thoughts, and feelings that perhaps don't yet exist in the public sphere, or at least have yet to be given names. Thus a glossary can be found at the back of the book.

In the following pages, you may find ideas and thoughts that you dislike, that you don't share, that jostle you, or that you reject entirely. You may equally find it dull and unoriginal. Either way, I must tell you that they are, to me, authentic, written in good faith, and I lay bare a facet of myself in the following pages that I have kept hidden for too long. I truly believe that, approached in the right way, we may yet make something healthy out of our sociopolitical systems. Perhaps even something built on kindness and empathy and respect towards others who are different from us; who like different things, or do things differently. Today many feel that the world stands on a cliff edge. It might be time to try something new because what we have – despite all of the beauty in the world – isn't working. Perhaps we should try something new, something that does work; not just for us but for everyone (and the world we live in).

Inquiry into Structural Problems in Political Progress

There are many concrete problems faced by humanity that have root causes in philosophical ideas. This inquiry starts from the premise that it is incumbent upon us to provide new frameworks for the understanding and solving of issues where thought has reached the limits of the paradigms that contextualise it.

Throughout history, political ideas and thought have had various sources, goals, and applications, many of which have been dubious in either intent or outcome. Whether it is the imposition of moral values upon societies, suffocating systems derived from metaphysical explanations of the universe, or the justification of repression, there has been more thought that constrains rather than frees humanity. Much about how to organise people rather than about how people could organise themselves. Many of the positive and healthier ideas that have come out of political thought have been reactions to this, and even those reactions regularly end up being equally or more unhealthy in the long run. Political ideas have, in many ways, ceased to contribute to the improvement of the human condition. We now need a phase where people help clean up the mess some philosophical ideas have caused in many areas of the human experience. This inquiry into the structural nature of our political ills serves as a starting point for exploration into the realm of both the creative unknown and the reformulation of well-trodden paths.

First, we seek to provide a framework for the understanding of the crisis faced by political ideas in the early 21st century by applying a lens borrowed from the philosophy of science to the history and nature of political representation by arguing that it exists within a Kuhnian paradigm. This paradigm has defined 'the political' and given meaning to the word we ultimately seek to redefine. It places key historical events as well as the present as being at varying points in phases of the paradigm. The dangers of the current era are discussed in context, as well as anomalous successes that suggest a way forward.

This is not an academic or theoretical work. It contains elements of theory but is more about exploring whether concepts from theory can be used as catalysts for concrete change. This is also in many ways a piece of janitorial work as it seeks to explain a mess. Not much in this inquiry is new. It is a reorganising of ideas and things that exist. My work is not academic but unashamedly imaginative. This essay forms the basis of several essays which attempt to imagine how our societies could look if only we were to make it so. It is about us all choosing to dare and create something that could be a chosen destiny.

KUHN: PARADIGMS, CRISIS, AND REVOLUTION

In 1962 Thomas Kuhn, an historian and philosopher of science, published his historic work on the nature of scientific development entitled *The Structure of Scientific*

*Revolutions.** His arguments were revolutionary and components of his outlook have since been absorbed across academic disciplines. Kuhn broke away from the traditional process of describing the history of science as a linear, incremental project, and proposed a structure that suggested an entirely different dynamic.

To Kuhn, science has phases where certain rules, norms, practices, or beliefs dominate a field for an extended period. These he called paradigms. A period where scientists share a sort of world view and an agreement about certain fundamentals within their given discipline. These, essentially, 'shape their world'. Within these paradigms, Kuhn argued, scientists theorise and experiment in their field in a given context, finding themselves solving problems and developing, irrespective of whether they are aware of the paradigm within which they operate.

Some of our very first scientific paradigms were created by a so-called 'Axis of Ancients'; namely, the ideas and works of Aristotle (4th century BCE), and Ptolemy and Galen (2nd century CE). Ptolemy was a Greek mathematician and thinker who lived in Alexandria in the 2nd century CE. His work on astronomy created one of the longest-lasting paradigms in science. Ptolemy's fundamental outlook was shaped by a stationary Earth at the centre of the universe. This was not out of keeping with the prevalent modes of thinking in his day and, more importantly, Ptolemy derived a mathematically coherent predictive model. This created a framework which was used and improved but left unchallenged into the 17th century because it was both useful, rigorous, and

* Thomas Kuhn, *The Structure of Scientific Revolutions* (University of Chicago Press, 1962)

functioned in accordance with the standards of the time as well as extremely useful within the limits within which it was required to operate. Galen was a Greek physician born in the 2nd century CE; a physician, surgeon, and philosopher who shaped notions of anatomy and medicine for over a millennium. Aristotle's physics, chemistry, and biology also shaped scientific outlooks for centuries. All three of these figures held immense weight and shaped paradigms in their respective fields well into the third quarter of the millennium. We have since abandoned many of their ideas and moved on.

Kuhn sought to explain the dynamics around the periods where scientific thought shifted and moved forwards to another mode of thinking and the reasons for these paradigm shifts. Scientific disciplines operating within a paradigm, Kuhn argued, reach a point of crisis. By crisis he meant a sort of 'dead end' for the logic and structure of a field. A point past which progress is to a great extent impeded by old and gradually weakening 'truths'. These crises are typified by several developments including anomalies in experimentation (new facts) that cannot be explained by the predominant theory. These anomalies appear in such a way (quantity and/or frequency) where they cannot be explained away by reasoning within the paradigm. Furthermore, new technologies allow for more detailed observations, data, or types of experiments, which call the entire paradigm into question. This makes the frameworks which were developed in the paradigm become increasingly inconsistent. Third, developments in other fields of science cross over and call into question established theories. Fourth, problems arise that cannot be answered within the framework of the existing paradigm.

The crisis of Ptolemean astronomy came in the 16th century with improvements in mathematics, observational equipment, and eventually the arrival of the telescope. Galen faced a crisis and was disproven by scientists and physicians who became more willing to experiment and observe the human body instead of relying on inherited ideas and works. Aristotle, who made what was perhaps one of the greatest (and lasting) contributions to science by way of framing the foundations of scientific reasoning, held many other scientific ideas and views that were equally abandoned or have been rethought almost entirely.

Kuhn argued that the response to crisis in science is what he called 'revolution', by which he meant the process through which we see the arrival of a new paradigm. The established paradigm is challenged by a new theory, which is either provable or gets accepted with time. This new paradigm changes the fundamental underpinnings of its discipline and old questions suddenly find answers. Old problems disappear by virtue of the change in the questions asked. Entirely new problems arise and are solved. A leap forward for the field in the shape of a new paradigm. Two modern examples of paradigm changes are Einstein's theories of relativity hammering the last nail into Newton's coffin and Darwin's theory of evolution which smashed socially sensitive notions of creation. With the Axis of Ancients, revolutions relegated their paradigms to history with the Copernican revolution replacing Ptolemy in astronomy, Vesalius' work replacing Galen in anatomy, and the works of Galileo and Newton giving birth to modern physics ending the Aristotelian dominance over many areas of science.

Kuhn revolutionised the way we look at the structure of scientific progress. Since Kuhn, the field has built on Kuhnian concepts and birthed rejections of his world view. The one thing few thinkers seem to disagree on is that there has been genuine progress in science and technology. Epistemological debates aside, progress in science is taken here as the field's ability to consistently challenge itself, asking and answering new questions. Progress in technology is the ability to provide tools for the furthering of scientific progress as well as improvements to the human condition.

There are two further points concerning Kuhn and his work that are relevant to us here. The first is his controversial notion of 'incommensurability'. Kuhn argued that the mindsets, methods of reasoning, and standards between two paradigms can be so different that when examining the same 'thing', scientists from different paradigms, having such a different basis of knowledge, would neither be seeing the same thing nor able to comprehend each other when describing something. Although the debate around this point in Kuhn's work is anything but fresh in the philosophy of science, it contains an important dimension that will be revisited later in this work. Kuhn argues that differences in language and meaning are a key obstacle when communicating across paradigms. By language, he means the meaning of concepts, ideas, and words in a given place, time, and discipline. For example, the word 'paradigm' was given an entirely new dimension and became widely used after Kuhn in both science and in general usage. He did not invent the word and yet his use of it has, to a certain extent, reshaped and deepened its meaning. Before 1962 few people had any conception of the meaning of paradigm. It was not in popular usage and those who did use it may have understood it differently. This should not be misconstrued as an argument for incommensurability (living in genuinely but not literally different worlds), but rather a simple acknowledgement of a small degree of 'untranslatability' around a specific word; an example of how distance across a short time span and mindset affects meaning. There is a reason that words augmented and expanded are added to the dictionary. The meaning of words can change and, indeed, are changing at an ever-increasing rate.

The second and final point about Kuhn's work is that his notion of the paradigm created a self-awareness about existing within them that was difficult to have before he described it. Since Kuhn's seminal work, three main developments have occurred. First, there has naturally been criticism and pushback against his notion from opposing schools of thought in the philosophy of science. These arguments have mainly centred around disagreements over the extent to which Kuhn was correct or incorrect in his analysis of the progress of science. The arguments do not suggest that the conceptual framework Kuhn developed was invalid as a tool of analysis irrespective of the case study or field at hand. Second, there has been much encouraging diversification of the use of Kuhnian paradigms, and other academic fields have benefited from his notion of the structure of progress. Third, the paradigm notion has occasionally suffered abuse. In these instances, the notion has been diluted to serve as a synonym of concepts such as 'point of view' or 'mindset'. This is not problematic when one takes into consideration the difference between a paradigm and a Kuhnian paradigm. The latter is a world view that is itself the context of an entire academic field and forms our fundamental outlook and experience of it.

Another crucial change which Kuhn's work has provided is that we are now more aware that we can exist within certain paradigms. This change in collective self-awareness shifts something fundamental about our experience of fields such as physics or biology, or a part of our lives, whether art or politics. In the same way as primitive societies were unable to see themselves as a culture within a context or world of other cultures, we live the 'truths' imposed by the constraints of being unable to see ourselves as existing within paradigms. Awareness of paradigms tells us that our existence is defined by the times we live in and our perceptions of our own pasts. That it is possible to be right today while knowing that we will be wrong tomorrow. It seemed that Newton was completely right, and yet the field has since moved on from many of his ideas while holding him in no less esteem.

THE SCIENTIFIC REVOLUTION AND A NEW HUMAN AVERAGE

For most of antiquity until the 16th century, the Axis of Ancients dominated almost every scientific field. The Scientific Revolution, starting with Copernicus, was a period in which the natural sciences (what is now physics, chemistry, and biology) all underwent their first major paradigm shift in over 1,500 years. The only member of the Axis to remain in vogue was Aristotle in the realm of politics, outside the scope of the natural sciences. By the beginning of the 18th century, Newton had become widely accepted, dealing the final blow to these old paradigms.

One of the biggest impacts of the Scientific Revolution was intellectual, social, and cultural progress on an unprecedented scale. It meant 'progress' in the modern sense of the word for the first time. A new meaning for an old word. The feeling of humanity moving 'forward' was entirely new. One of the main catalysts of this change was the technological innovation of the printing press. Although printing had an established tradition, Gutenberg's wooden press of 1568 was a game changer. It allowed for a significant reduction in cost and an increase in the number of books that could be printed and published, making reading increasingly accessible and allowing scientific (and other) ideas to disseminate into society in unprecedented ways. Without being conscious of the process, humanity harnessed technology to change itself forever.

The Scientific Revolution can also be read as a point of departure for our species. A time where we broke through the cloud of dogma to challenge the very foundations of our knowledge and existence. Not just at the highest level of scientific thought but progressing towards a new 'human average'. The average person's quality of life, literacy levels, and ability to process and interact with ideas were pushed forward by science and technology. We progressed for the first time, adding meaning to the term 'Early Modern Period'.

The incredible transition initiated by the Scientific Revolution is described by David Wootton in his book, *The Invention of Science.*

> *A typical well-educated European in 1600 [...] believes in witches [...] werewolves [...] believes Circe really did turn Odysseus's crew into pigs. He believes mice are spontaneously generated in piles of straw [...] has seen a unicorn's horn but not a unicorn. He believes that a murdered body will bleed in the presence of the murderer [...] He believes the shape, colour and texture of a plant can be a clue to how it will work as a medicine because God*

> *designed nature to be interpreted by mankind [...] He believes that nature abhors a vacuum [...] He believes of course that the Earth stands still and the sun and stars turn around the Earth once every 24 hours [...] He believes that Aristotle (4th century* BCE*) is the greatest philosopher who ever lived, and that Pliny (1st century* CE*), Galen and Ptolemy (both 2nd century* CE*) are the best authorities on natural history, medicine, and astronomy.*[*]

Wootton contrasts this description with that of a similarly educated European in 1733.

> *Our Englishman has looked through a telescope and a microscope; he owns a pendulum clock and a stick barometer – and he knows there is a vacuum at the end of a tube. He does not know anyone who believes in witches, werewolves, magic, alchemy, or astrology; he thinks the Odyssey is fiction not fact. He is confident that the unicorn is a mythical beast. He does not believe that the shape or colour of a plant has any significance for an understanding of its medical use. He believes that no creature large enough to be seen by the naked eye is generated spontaneously [...] He believes that the Earth goes round the sun. He knows that the rainbow is produced by refracted light [...] He knows the heart is a pump.*[†]

* David Wootton, *The Invention of Science* (Penguin, 2016) pp. 6–7

† Ibid., pp. 10–11

As put by Wootton, there had been a 'complete destruction of the Aristotelian distinction between heavens and the Earth'.[*] A true scientific revolution with permanent implications for humanity's condition and intellectual development. It is important to note that these descriptions are those of an intellectual elite, well above the human average. Since then, not only have scientific ideas advanced but there has been a significant democratisation of human knowledge and intellectual development in many fields.

PRODUCTS AND PROGRESS IN SCIENCE

Here we seek to define the words 'product' and 'progress' within the context of this essay. A reason words need defining is that different people understand them differently whether the gap is across space, time, both, and even paradigm. The act of description defines, and definition controls meaning. There exists of course a debate to be had around the nature of the science-technology dynamic and how they interact; whether there would have been a Galileo without the telescope, so to speak. This discussion lies outside the scope of this work.

Products are understood to be the 'products' or 'things' that a field of human inquiry contributes to the human experience. The definition has neither a positive nor negative connotation. For example, products of science are things like the telescope, penicillin, GPS, the Internet, guns, nuclear energy, and weapons. It is noted that some of these things are given to science to use rather than being derived from it, but this

* Ibid., p. 7

debate is for another forum. Furthermore, not all products of science are physical. Many of the most important products relate to ideas and mindsets. For example, the notion that knowledge can be verified is included in our definition of a product of science.

Progress here is defined as having two core components, both of which must be at work for a field to be progressing. First, the field must consistently provide products that improve the human experience and thereby pull up the human average over an extended period. Second, progress requires the ability for a field to move into new paradigms and to answer new questions within those paradigms. So, in Kuhnian terms, progress is the ability to solve problems within the paradigm, reach a point of crisis, and shift into a new paradigm as a new phase of advancement is the second element required for progress.

Science and politics push and pull each other. Sometimes they hold each other back. For science, the sociopolitical context is key because it defines what we do with the tools we make and the things we learn; or, in more graphic terms, whether the axe fells a tree or chops off a head. Historically, politics also exerted influence over the rate of scientific progress. But today, context defines science's purpose and not whether it can progress at all. To a certain extent, science has broken free of many political constraints and left politics behind in its ability to progress from paradigm to paradigm. Many paradigms in politics are entrenched or, as it were, still controlled by the fundamentals of its Axis of Ancients.

PARADIGMS IN POLITICS: THE REPRESENTATIONAL PARADIGM

The nature of political representation makes up the foundation stone of an entire Kuhnian paradigm in politics. That politics itself or a facet of it is ruled by a Kuhnian paradigm is the central thesis of this essay. It is indeed possible that we live in a first 'ancient' paradigm, the shedding of which this book seeks to help initiate. The question is how to see a primordial political paradigm when existing inside it, considering that Kuhn only saw them in science once humanity had passed through several. This movement, from one step to another, allows us to observe change as we look back at ourselves and the history of our ideas and achievements in science. Kuhn's work has the added benefit of opening the door for us to see what has yet to move. His work, as well as that of others, has provided the framework as well as much of the groundwork for identifying paradigms in places where we may not have expected to find them.

Many things in politics evolve, but a paradigm frames the fundamentals of that discipline and area of the human experience. There is a deeply entrenched constant that governs something which could be a constraint on a potential future: a law or truth that underpins everything. The nature of political representation is something so basic that, if reshaped, would change an entire facet of our humanity.

THREE STRAND POLITICS: REPRESENTATION – ORGANISATION – LANGUAGE

Here we will look at three fundamental strands of politics: representation, organisation, and language. Politics is to a great extent defined by the nature, evolution, and interplay of the three. Most other facets of politics are either qualities or subsets of (or are defined by) these three. Representation (R) is ruled by a paradigm, which we will call the Representational Paradigm (RP). It permeates the other two and is, therefore, the defining feature of politics as we understand it. Our RP is the most important, long-term political paradigm. We live in the first RP or RP1.

PARADIGMS IN POLITICS: THE REPRESENTATIONAL PARADIGM

We live in a first ancient paradigm that has remained a constant throughout human history and we have yet to shed it and move on to a second. We live in a Kuhnian paradigm in which we are represented, politically, by 'others'. This means that we neither represent ourselves directly nor do we lack R entirely. Whether we select our representatives or have them imposed on us is but a nuance when we look at the issue in the broadest framework possible.

What does it mean that 'the nature of political representation makes up an entire Kuhnian paradigm in politics', and that 'we live in a paradigm where we are represented by 'others'? How are we to catch sight of the fabric of our context? There are two paths to follow. The first is to make a case for it. The second is by understanding that we seek something that might only be seen if we imagine it and to follow through with attempting to describe it. The search for progress in politics will require a rethinking of fundamental political concepts and a new paradigm. The ideas put forward in section two of this book require a framework both to develop and understand them. This section is an outline of this lens.

> By Representation we mean what *we* mean, not what *it* means.
>
> Being in a Kuhnian paradigm is a binary state. We are either in it or we are not.
>
> Either there is no representation or there is.
>
> When there is no R, $R=0$ (absolute state).
>
> When there is R, $0<R$ (intermediate state or absolute state).
>
> Within $0<R$ there are two further possible states:
>
> Representation by others: $0<R<1$ (intermediate state);
>
> Self-representation: $R=1$ (absolute state).

RP1

'R' is the letter we will use to portray the level of equitable distribution of political representation among individuals of a given group. It is expressed in terms of units on a scale of 0 to 1. This is an illustrative tool. A low R means highly unequal distribution of political representation, and a higher R means a more equal distribution. Many factors, among them representatives, have an impact on R. They can cause it to be increased or decreased, but there cannot be representatives if $R=1$.

There are three potential states. This does not entail a value judgement or a statement of desire or even possibility in the practical sense, but rather an observation that there are three potential states of being. We live in RP1, where $0<R<1$.

Our current paradigm can also be described as individuals being represented on a scale of $0<R<1$.

Historically there has been a general trend of gradual migration from 0 towards 1. For example, an absolute monarchy could be described as 0.1 or 0.2, or even 0.3, and modern Switzerland as 0.5, 0.6, or 0.7. This notion is conceptual. Developing a methodology for calculation will affect R scores. There may be disagreement around the criteria for data selection to evaluate R. There may be even more disagreement on the methodology to apply and the results will therefore vary. Irrespective of methodology, we find that $0<R<1$; that is, that our paradigm is our political context itself and permeates the fabric of our world. The RP has also been consistent throughout human history.

$R=1$ means fully equitable, direct, (self) representation on all issues that relate to a group, something we have yet to witness. That would be a new Kuhnian paradigm.

$R=0$ means no Representation at all, even indirect, because one person, even an absolutist king, represents himself and his subjects indirectly through the advancement of interests and through societal structures that afford some a degree of R.

Millions of people have suffered the abhorrent personal and group tragedy of $R=0$ throughout human history. Two examples:

1. Person A is a slave. Person A is not represented as they are classified as property so R=0. Person B is Person A's master. Person B enjoys $0<R<1$;
2. Person A has a number tattooed onto their arm as they get off a train: R=0.

Despite the horrors that humanity is capable of inflicting upon itself as it 'others' individuals and groups (R=0), which has been the reality of millions, this does not make up a historical paradigm in the Kuhnian sense of the definition. These people are removed from the political sphere and by this process of exclusion we get a glimpse of what R=0 could look like under some distant (and increasingly possible) futuristic scenarios.

An RP is defined by the nature of the mode of political representation of a time. This means that there is a fundamental defining feature to political representation that has been consistent throughout the paradigm. For R to be part of a truly Kuhnian paradigm it needs to be global in nature, pervasive, and enduring, and have a constant that has shaped this strand of politics.

Our search for the RP looks at one core question, 'who represents people politically?' or, 'how are people represented politically?' The answer is that in this paradigm we are represented by others. Whether voluntarily or not, we delegate political responsibilities to representatives. These include executive decisions and administration, legislation, and oversight. Representation can be seen as something quantifiable and distinctive from self-representation. Self-representation would entail the individual representing themselves on such matters. In a sociohistorical context, it would mean taking R away from representatives. The degree to which an individual from a given group is under-represented (or even over-represented) can be seen through the lens of ascribing an R value. If all actions where political interests are represented were described as either votes or vote equivalents, we would find that some individuals are either under- or over-represented. Whether we elect representatives or have them imposed upon us are factors which affect the equitable distribution of political representation. This is done with varying levels of competence and success.

So the question is, 'if we are represented by others, how do we describe the extent to which representation is equitable?' Equitable is an unachievable goal in our paradigm by virtue of its nature. With representatives, one does not represent oneself. The R of a group by a representative automatically subsumes the individual. When we elect a representative they are sometimes seen as representing the individuals within the group by virtue of their representation of the group as a whole. The fact is that they are usually representing broad notions of political ideas that the group has chosen them to represent, or specific interests, whether unrelated or on behalf of a segment of the group. Everyone voting freely for representatives does not mean $R=1$, it is just a modus operandi among others within the context of $0<R<1$.

A fully equitable system of governance would allow an individual a full vote or vote equivalent over relevant facets of the political. This suggests the rethinking of representatives in the way that we understand them today because representation via others automatically subsumes personal vote. Voting 'on your behalf' can never truly fully represent the variances in views among constituents.

Take, for example, a democratic parliamentary system of governance. Something that in the early 21st century was seen as being a paragon of successful R. A representative of a geographical area or group is elected by constituents to represent them on a national stage. This means that one person represents a group in front of a larger group. The individual's vote is subsumed post representative selection. It is assumed that they will be represented. Even if all voters of the given district share the same broad political views (which is impossible), there is no space for nuance. We see that even in a modern democratic parliamentary system, the nature of R is the source of its inequitable distribution. It is the fact that someone represents 'you' or 'your group' (a potentially arbitrary grouping) that is the source of the inequality. The notion that the constituents who voted for the losing candidate should lose even a degree of R is merely a product of having candidates in the first place. Those who backed the 'winning' candidate are only slightly better served.

Another example would be a contemporary dictatorship where unelected officials are selected to represent districts in a national parliament that is tightly controlled via centralised mechanisms. Seen through the lens of RP1 or $0<R<1$, this mode of R is merely a less equitable version of a democratic parliamentary system. The argument that one might be 'fair' and the other 'not fair' because of the difference in representative selection methods is merely a symptom of an observer trapped in the paradigm because that argument focuses on representative selection methods as a source of legitimacy. The truth is that they are both inequitable and lie relatively close together on a broader spectrum of distribution of political representation.

PHASES OF RP1

Sometimes there is value in cutting broad timelines into smaller chunks. This is especially useful when the RP is the only one we have ever had. Describing our current paradigm as having existed 'since forever' isn't particularly efficient, nor does it allow us to reflect on changes or trends within the paradigm. It is also worth noting that while $0<R<1$, things have moved along the spectrum when one takes the long view. Not for everyone, all the time, and everywhere, but perhaps enough that we could make the claim that our RP has had two main phases along with sub-phases. The first we will call the 'Absolutist phase' and the second, that of higher R and generally seen as starting around the time of the French and American revolutions, we will call the 'Bridge phase'. This does not exclude the possibility of having different frameworks through which to view our RP, but rather that it relates to the themes and topics that will be explored in the coming essays.

THE ABSOLUTIST PHASE

The concept of the RP relates to the fundamental nature of political representation within a given group. Before the French Revolution, political representation (anomalies such as Athenian democracy and god kings aside) constituted representation by the absolute king or ruler for most political systems. They either embodied the state, were the state, or a combination thereof. This was the ultimate disproportionate political representation vis-à-vis the total sum of humans within a political entity. If you imagine a group of 100,000 people who have, between them, a theoretical total of 100,000 units of possible political representation (votes and vote equivalents), an absolute monarchy like that of Louis XIV would have most of the 100,000 units allocated to one person or a few families, hence the ultimate inequality of R. This low R value was the historical norm in most places for most of human history, with higher levels of R being anomalous.

The Absolutist phase coincided, generally, with the era before the arrival of the printing press, where the development (educational, political) of the average human was low. Thus they were neither fully represented nor could they represent themselves adequately. This phase also coincided, generally, with the pre-Copernican era, where science had yet to 'take off' and leave behind Aristotle, Ptolemy, and Galen, the Axis of Ancients who had dominated scientific thought for the first two-thirds of the last two millennia. The 16th and 17th centuries saw the advent of Copernicus, Newton and, more importantly for this discussion, Gutenberg's printing press. Scientific and technological revolution. New paradigms in science and new tools for human progress. As the 18th century proceeded, the human average shifted with more people learning to read, sparking the end of the phase heralded by events such as the French Revolution. After this event, the distribution of political representation changed and humanity progressed towards the second phase of our RP. Absolutism as the norm in the paradigm was dying as R increased, but the fundamental nature of political representation stayed the same.

THE BRIDGE AND THE INVENTION OF POLITICAL BELIEF

The Bridge phase is the bridge between our Absolutist past and the future of tomorrow. Whether that future is a third phase of the current RP or the beginning of another paradigm altogether could be a matter of choice as well as imperative. The Bridge is characterised by the fact that the degree of representational inequality that was so pronounced in the Absolutist phase became less intense. More people represented others. Elected or unelected officials represented groups and citizens by extension and did so as a matter of policy. Parliaments, congresses, Dumas, *Assemblees Nationales*, political parties, and associations, etc. Along with it has come an entire political language which defines the structure of our political thoughts and interactions. It permeates our everyday life to such an extent that it is part of the fabric of our cultures and we don't always recognise it. Colours like red and blue carry intrinsic meaning. Directions like left and right are words heavy with emotion. The language of the Bridge is our linguistic culture, in much the same way that the language of piety soaked Western political culture during the Middle Ages. The meaning of the words we use define us and we are bound by the political language that we speak. The difference between the people of the Bridge and those of the 13th century is that we are, on occasion, able to observe ourselves in the third person and assess our place within a sociohistorical context. The Bridge has been successful in having a generally less disproportionate level of inequality of R; something reached by the early 1990s with the fall of the USSR. Here the 100,000 units are spread less disproportionately than in the first phase of the paradigm but reach nowhere near the position of one human to one 'unit' of R, even in modern representative democracies.

This is where most of humanity stands today, somewhere on the scale of R via others (in the language of the Bridge:

politicians). Some places have democracies, some don't, but almost all nations today claim to represent their citizens via officials, politicians, parties, and assemblies. The Bridge is part of a global paradigm, just like Absolutism was its first incarnation before the French Revolution. A key point is that it was enabled by technologies such as the printing press, which brought humankind forwards with it and accelerated the development of humanity. Political representation is more equal, but not yet truly equal and is the defining characteristic of the first paradigm. Furthermore, the main failure of the Bridge phase is its persistent inability to successfully develop globally acceptable answers to political questions via its favourite framework: modern political belief.

ORGANISATION

Organisation is a strand of politics defined to a large extent by the RP. It is a product of grouping, and grouping forms the basis of Organisation (O) and can be either arbitrary (such as a nation-state), or voluntary (such as individuals joining political parties). Different modes of O lead to certain norms of R although it has never changed R's fundamental mode. Organisation is not dominated by an overarching paradigm, but rather there are various modes and levels of O. These can be divided into three main classes. The first is 'how individuals group'; second is 'how these groups organise'; and third is 'how they interact'.

Within these subsets there have been paradigms and some may still exist. For the second, the nation-state is a key defining feature of the global system of organisation in the early 21st century, but not necessarily the defining feature with which individuals identify. Whether it is a paradigm or not depends on definition. On the one hand, it could be argued that it is a paradigm because almost 100% of humans are citizens of a state. In this argument, all the tribal, party, racial, ideological lines, and others are assumed to be subsumed either totally or enough to be less relevant factors. This is not something that is consistently the case and therefore undermines the suggestion that the nation-state constitutes a Kuhnian paradigm despite its prevalence. Furthermore, with increasing migration and displacement, the number of people who are either stateless or reside 'temporarily' in new geographies is in many places becoming increasingly untenable for both the resources of host countries and the feelings of their electorates. The argument against the nation-state constituting a paradigm is that many 'subnational' facets of political organisation are, in fact, supranational and more defining to the individuals that make up a group, that is, a more important form of affiliation. Some examples of this are Spanish regions with secessionist tendencies, while others are an affiliation to the international ideological dimension of contemporary right-wing nationalism. The fluctuating nature of interplay between these types of affiliations, as well as the inability of the state to subsume them all consistently over an extended period, would indicate that nation-states are not a paradigm in the Kuhnian sense, but a significant part of a package of different overlapping modes of O.

The global system of inter-state interaction in the late 20th and early 21st centuries has been part of a loose Organisational Paradigm (OP). This paradigm is the notion that states should subscribe to a system that governs and regulates their interactions and some of their internal functions.

The United Nations, despite its many failures, can be seen as representative of the notion that groups should subscribe to a method of interaction, governed by rules. This is a step further than bilateral treaties and group alliances, which dominated the structure of the world prior to the First World War. The current system and the notion of subscription to a system are in crisis. If indeed it is an OP, it may prove to be short-lived.

Historically, imperialism was arguably an OP. The period where the British, Spanish, Portuguese, German and French empires reigned encompassed enough of the globe's population to subsume other modes of political organisation, action, and association, thereby becoming a paradigm. This is no longer the case, nor should we seek to recreate such systems considering the despicable nature of many of their facets such as violence, slavery, and resource and heritage exploitation.

Are political parties a current political paradigm? Although a symptom of the Bridge, their pervasiveness does not automatically mean that they constitute a paradigm. Parties are better described as the dominant mode of ideological grouping, with implications for the distribution of R.

None of the above are overriding OPs in the early 21st century. There exist various facets to O, all of which are defined by their existence within the current RP. So O has several strands. Some strands could be paradigms but there is currently no overriding OP.

LANGUAGE

*The meaning of a word is its use in the language.**

Wittgenstein

Language is the third strand of politics. It is a tool and is used in a game in the political sense which, like many games, is won by the successful control of territory. Academic fields, politicians, people, and ideas vie for domination over the meaning of words within and across groups. They define and control them whether they are conscious of it or not. This game is a third strand of politics: language and its control. It is not time that alters the meaning of words, but forces acting over time.

The meaning of words is defined by how they are used in a sentence as well as the context within which the sentence is used.

Consider the word 'sick'. Such a simple word has space for misinterpretation. 'This is sick' could have very different meanings. Just as could 'he is so sick'. Sentences where understanding runs from the extreme expression of disgust to admiration. Our perception of the context of the sentence will define which of the possible meanings we are to infer. Some will only see one possible meaning irrespective of context because they are bound to theirs. Seeing context differently changes how we understand a word or sentence.

Consider the following political statement: 'He is as blue as a donkey.' This statement will seem entirely nonsensical to anyone unfamiliar with late 20th/early 21st-century American

---

* Wittgenstein, Ludwig, *Philosophical Investigations*, trans. P. M. S. Hacker, G. E. M. Anscombe, and Joachim Schulte (Wiley, 2009)

politics. The initiated or American will in turn understand the sentence by virtue of the association of the colour blue and the donkey symbol with the Democratic Party. So the statement means that 'this person is a supporter of the American Democratic Party in the 20th or early 21st century'. And yet the person interpreting the statement will protest that the formulation of the sentence is quite outlandish and probably ridiculous. It sounds weird and is awkward, but this is because it is not in popular use. This tells us that popular use can affect not just meaning but reception, that is, what a group understands the meaning of something to be and how we are used to using it.* The dissemination of political phrases, terms, and notions is key to the control of both the political language that permeates our experience of the field as well as the definition of what does or does not belong to the political.

Another example of politics appropriating words is the use of the directions 'left' and 'right'. Words deep with significance and a source of strong emotions and, regularly, violence. Enemies are made by virtue of the meaning imputed to left and right. Words have been appropriated into terms. These have meanings beyond the function of the original word. All of this can and does change. The question is why and how should this be done consciously? There is an entire political language that is sometimes imperceptible because of its pervasiveness. It controls our world and changing it could alter our understanding of the basic notion of intergroup interaction.

The meaning of a word can provide insight into place and time. But can you understand it outside its context, or is

* Ibid., p. 32

there what Kuhn referred to as 'untranslatability'? An understanding of a word but not its meaning to another person from a different time. The three words 'fuck a sheep' once described an activity that had nothing to do with intercourse and rather a lot to do with shearing. And yet now the notion is abhorrent to (hopefully) everyone.

Changes in the meaning of words have an 'initiator'. This is a person or group that appropriates a word. Control of more words means more power and the ability to convince others of an idea or mode of thought.

The act of description defines. Redefining and creating new words changes things. It can cause notions and ideas to cease to exist and others to be born. What do we want to relegate to a previous era, part of an old paradigm? It is for us to initiate, appropriate, and create. These essays are in part about using current organisation and language to shift R to 1 (a new paradigm) to in turn reshape O into a new paradigm. We are searching for an OP where R=1 because equality of R is the true source of real equality.

A PARADIGM-FREE DEFINITION OF POLITICS?

How could politics be defined if our thoughts were not bound by any mode, era, or paradigm?

We could say, 'it is the nature of the interactions that occur when humans group'. Or one could ask, 'how does that definition reflect my understanding of politics as I know it?' To which we could answer, 'it doesn't, it just tells you how deeply politics has been shaped by the RP and hints at the breadth of possibilities if we lived in another'.

The End of the Bridge

...toxins left by the rank spume of an epoch's storm waves.

Stefan Zweig*

A PARADIGM IN CRISIS

The ends of paradigms, according to Kuhn, have two main characteristics: crises (the paradigm eventually stops working as it should) and anomalies (cases that defy the paradigm and show us that things could work differently). Our Representational Paradigm (RP) is in crisis and is at a turning point and contains important anomalies. We are reaching the end of the Bridge. Humanity has reached a crossroads where we either seize what could be our only window of opportunity for equality or we stand to lose the gains we have made since the end of Absolutism.

The crisis of our RP started with the sociopolitical events and changes that came in the wake of the Industrial Revolution in the 19th century. This is not to say that all subsequent

* Stefan Zweig, *Montaigne* (Pushkin Press, 2015) p. 49

events emanate directly from it, but that it can be taken as a convenient starting date for some of the disturbances we have endured in the ensuing 150 years. Here we focus on the problematic ideas of nationalism, fascism, communism, and top-down globalism as sharing common threads which are themselves symbolic of the end-of-paradigm crisis. Namely, political ideas as solutions and the promotion of the perceived collective interest over individuals and their freedoms. Six selected examples among many help to demonstrate this. There are dozens more that could also be named.

NATIONALISM: 'BELIEF IN A GROUP'

Grouping is the first step to Organisation (O). Nationalism, by virtue of its arbitrary and exclusive grouping mechanisms, is by nature a conflict-generating idea. It is also something that has evolved and changed with time, but its fundamentals have remained essentially the same. The notion that a state or government should organise individuals and groups into a 'whole' while posing as a reflection or protector of identity to the exclusion of others contains the idea that the nation is a representative or source of identity.

Nationalism as an idea has played a historical role in moving us out of the extreme hierarchies and distortions of Representation (R) from which we suffered under Absolutism where sun kings, god kings, and even petty kings abounded. But nationalism, while remaining respectful of its early successes in redistributing R, is not good enough for today's world, especially considering both its role in the disasters of the 20th century and the increasing multiculturalism of Western societies. It is a leftover concept of a time of revolutions and within it holds all the anger and bloodthirstiness of an era that needed to free itself from nations where the sovereign was the law, state, and its dignity. Today, nationalism's continuing grip on politics and thought surrounding it means that the world is unable to progress into a more advanced stage of both R and O. The crisis we face at the end of the Kuhnian paradigm is that nationalism has hindered the arrival of larger and more inclusive structures. This has, historically, played a positive role in standing against monistic globalism such as communism, but it has also led to extreme nationalism and may be standing in the way of new ideas that could help us progress. Could it be that it is impeding the development of a freer, fairer future rooted in something else that nationalism cannot allow without passing away into the dustbin that is our past?

The nation represents individuals by default and subsumes them. Conversely, the idea that nation-states are the modern reflections of 'natural' or 'eternal' groupings does not hold. This is not just for members of minorities but also for individuals who are constituents of what is defined as the 'majority group'.

So then why is it that members of the majority can feel subsumed or oppressed in a nationalistic sociopolitical environment? Everyone is part of a minority on some issue or fact, just possibly not on one of the things that current structures emphasise as being exclusive and so some people may feel it less than others. But with enough nationalism, everyone eventually feels it on some topic and the significant negative impact it has on their lives. What they then experience is what conventional 'minorities' feel all the time on the most important things that define them. It is our definition of minority within the sociopolitical context that allows us to get to such a point.

Fatherland, motherland, and homeland are ideas we feel and feed that aren't real. That does not make them a bad thing but translating this identity into an arbitrary grouping such as a nation-state is where the expression of feeling takes the wrong route. It is not because the majority group believes that all feel included, nor is it necessarily real for anyone in the group, but also minority groups feel endangered by it. And everyone is part of some minority. If you take together the ideas, races, religions, values, issues, notions that in total could constitute a minority, in many cases one might find themselves looking at over 30% and in some cases, outright majorities. At this point, an individual almost always holds at least one view or opinion in which they are part of a minority. 'Modern' groupings (nation-states) necessarily mean you are always part of a minority for something. And if it is for something major, like race, religion, or ethnicity, you are a minority that suffers more than people who are considered part of a majority but are really members of minorities on smaller issues. No person is fully represented under the current forms of O.

The nation-state is fundamentally exclusive by nature while posing, in its milder forms, as inclusive because of representative democracy or minority rights enshrined in law. The law protecting a minority doesn't necessarily mean they fit into the grouping. It means that their lives 'should be relatively okay' without automatically providing the structures that allow them the quality of life and rights to which they are entitled by law. Suggesting that (the nation-state) groups would lose their identity without it and its physical incarnation does not necessarily have to be true. The idea of losing one's identity due to organisational or representational change is indeed something to fear, but fear of something does not make it true. A lack of visible alternatives, on the other hand, necessarily cements fears and gives the construct the appearance of permanence and need for protection of what seems to be natural or eternal groupings, but which are merely reflections of an arbitrary group. There needs to be a method of grouping which allows the individual to maintain their integrity in all facets of themselves. This will only happen after we shed the notion of the necessity for a 'cohesive whole' as a nation-state and subscribe to new methods of O and R.

When we take the long view of history, the notion of arbitrary grouping leads to extreme nationalism and from there regularly to barbarism and the most dreadful version of the 'ideas as a solution' framework. Fascism and genocide are what is probably the most sickening crisis of the Bridge, and yet they are merely an extension of what appear to be milder foundational roots.

'SOLUTIONS' – FASCISM

While nationalism has played a role in hindering the arrival of new modes of R and O in the 21st century, it has also had products of its own. Fascism is the extreme product of the Bridgeist concept of nationalism, as it is understood in the modern sense of the term. It is part of the most extreme behaviour the end-of-Bridge crisis has witnessed. A relatively recent product, its most vicious incarnation was Hitler's Nazi Germany. It has existed in various forms since then, many of which are still present and resurge regularly under various guises. In its complete form, it is the ultimate subsuming of the individual for the collective notion of state and nation. Fascism is also presented (sometimes effectively) as a set of beliefs that are 'solutions' to certain perceived problems and grievances that arise when nation-states fail to achieve certain outcomes for their populations. This 'political idea as solution' mindset is typical of the Bridge where humanity has been trained to seek solutions to all-encompassing problems in political thought, with fascism being an extreme extension of commonly held mind-sets. In fascism, there are solutions to 'problems' caused by minorities, foreigners, immigration, and any types of 'other' that the nation-state excludes by virtue of its foundational ideas: namely, that a nation is a natural group that has identifiable characteristics in a specific geography to the exclusion of others. Fascism corresponds not only with reduced rights for certain groups within the larger grouping, but the implementation of laws of mechanisms of governance which impinge on the freedoms and livelihoods of such groups to such a degree that nationalism devolves into barbarism and terrorism. The fact that there is a discernible line between the two does not make milder nationalism acceptable. Nationalism in comparison to fascism always manages to appear civilised despite it being the precursor of the latter.

It is not only minorities that are affected by nationalism and fascism. The majority that tends to vote in a fascist regime finds itself suffocated over time. No space for nuance within the majority, no dissent, and no alternative thought, no matter how slight and well-intentioned the deviation. This leads to the suffocation and subjugation of the majority whose ideals it claims to represent. Everyone eventually finds themselves a minority on some issue and the price paid by each individual in a fascist state is high because the individual has no inherent status above the nation. No dignity for themselves and no rights other than to endure a 'collective will' imposed by an elite posing as representative. All of this can be reduced to a 'decrease in R'.

The solution mindset also leads to 'final solutions'. The horrors of the Holocaust are something we should never forget. Terrorism is sometimes only two steps away from a nationalist government, and one step away from a fascist regime. Things can all too quickly devolve into murder, ethnic cleansing, or even genocide against targeted groups. There have been many smaller scale instances of such atrocities around the world since the 1940s. Nationalistic governments that cross over the line into fascism, whether on a specific issue or in entirety, have been a recurrent theme throughout the 20th and early 21st centuries. Genocide is not a 'sign' of fascism but rather the ultimate consequence of it. Fascism does not require all the Nazi trappings to be identified as something to fear, despise, and stand up against.

'SOLUTIONS' – COMMUNISM

The second pronounced and disastrous example of the Bridgeist notion of 'political ideas as a solution' mindset is communism. A failed globalist project, communism was a major political paradigm contender for much of the 20th century. Much like fascism, it is collectivist, with no space for the individual and little room for nuance, yet it plays a very different function at the end of a Kuhnian paradigm in crisis. Communism can be seen as the first significant globalist idea that attempts to move past nationalism and the antiquated conception of the nation. It is, in that narrow but important sense, a precursor of the European Union (EU) and other supranational systems.

It is one of the most interesting Bridgeist ideas because it is a pure and unashamed construct (although it did contain foul elements of historicism and historical inevitability). This is not a value judgement, but rather the observation of a theoretical framework around which millions of humans have rallied with practical and philosophical implications, and which has contended with other modes of O to gain supremacy. This was entirely unique in human history and has set a precedent worth noting.

The reasons for communism's failure, seen through the lens of this essay, are threefold. First, it is a political idea as understood in the Bridgeist sense and so presented as a solution to be 'believed' in and 'followed'. Second, it looked at the various political and socioeconomic groups of the world and assumed that an ideology could impose things 'from above' under the guise of being grassroots for the good of the whole. This implies that what is different should become the same and that the arbitrary grouping of all humans under a belief system is both possible and desirable. This meant that it grouped arbitrarily rather than finding modes of O that allowed groups to coexist and for individuals to be free to develop, evolve, and grow. It has neither freed the individual nor does it hold the notion of a single person's value at its core. The cost in lives has been unbelievably high. Third, at its core lies a prescription of economic medicine.

While credit must be given to ideas that reject parochialism, beliefs which are about morals, imposition, and peoples rather than liberty, choice, and individuals, add little value to humanity's emancipation and development.

TOP-DOWN GLOBALISM

The 'globalism' of the second half of the 20th century and the first decade of the 21st is a pragmatic product of an elitist conception of governance mechanisms and beliefs. This statement has nothing to do with the conspiracy theories that abound regarding global governance mechanisms which do not deserve further mention. What we are saying here is that in the aftermath of the two world wars, several unique things happened. First, there was a decision that a mode of global governance should be pursued while respecting the sovereignty of nation-states. Hence the birth of the League of Nations and its successor, the United Nations, both of which can be characterised as systems of intergroup interaction. Furthermore, global trade became increasingly 'globalised', with complex results for which this is not the appropriate forum for discussion. The crises of these two systems (the rules of inter-state interaction and global trade) of the early 21st century demonstrate that neither the grouping method nor the mode of interaction are able to achieve their goals and possibly will not be able to withstand phases of failure.

The EU, a product of the same elites that conceived the United Nations, has reached a similar phase. Incapable of respecting the integrity of groupings and unable to get people to evolve past them, the EU as a mechanism of regional governance has come back to clash with nationalism in the second decade of the 21st century. Increasingly, right-wing governments are threatening its integrity; with it, liberty may die. And yet the EU as a guarantor of certain standards of governance is not an acceptable long-term mechanism for populations. Neither direction is the solution they seek or promise to be.

Why then is globalism's second start (the first being communism) dangerous? One of the main reasons is its source. Groups of men (historically to the systematic exclusion of women), many of them well-intentioned but above a certain age and with a certain level of status, thought on people's behalf and imposed a system of governance upon the world that has failed to achieve its goals. Many of these goals are noble and yet the source of the decision-making is key to defining the nature of the project and the structure imposed upon populations. Second, this source of decision-making has undermined the legitimacy and sustainability of the project. Representatives are an increasingly outdated notion in a world where the nation-state is not the only mode of grouping as people can now communicate, assemble, debate, and vote online.

AMERICAN DEMOCRACY

The United States of America presents the archetype of both the successes and crises of the Bridge; the successes and failures of systems of O where people represent others. America has been incredibly successful on several levels. It has worked better than most at overall wealth creation and maintaining a relatively high level of liberty, freedom, and equality for its majority group. The above rights for minorities are also, to a certain extent, enshrined in the law. This is recent and their application in practice is still far from successful. There are of course no guarantees that the progress of the last 70 years will be furthered or maintained.

Failure is at hand when it comes to maintaining their system of separation of powers. It is becoming increasingly pronounced in the mechanisms of governance that allow for freedoms and liberties to be eroded without the direct consent of the population. Something we are seeing in the 21st century in many nations across the globe. This is a core weakness of representative democracy in general. If people must protest at all, it means that the system isn't truly government for the people by the people, because a people in charge don't need to protest. Although they are failing to uphold their representative democracy according to their own standards, they did not invent that method of governance and may have implemented it better than most nations despite the national psychosis that they appear to have been experiencing since 2016.

America's greatest failure from an international perspective lies in their defeat at promoting their system of governance on a global scale. American democracy has been, by nature, expansionist. It has consistently undertaken to 'bring freedom' through various means and its system is a globally ambitious idea. Globalist in its intentions, representative democracy as exported by decades of American administrations has been incapable of attracting and convincing entire populations to become a Kuhnian paradigm. Economic and military power have allowed for groups to be cajoled into structures that imitate the trappings but not the spirit of representative democracy. It is a weak paradigm contender. This failure is becoming increasingly pronounced today and is putting the entire world at risk of being undermined by groups with regressive values. It is not so much that their ideas (at least on the spectrum of Bridgeist ideas) are necessarily bad, but rather that forced application of American political values has been rejected in too many places.

LEADERLESS REVOLUTIONS IN BETWEEN

The early 21st century has seen a set of 'leaderless' and often 'failed' revolutions, a prime example being the Egyptian Revolution of 2011 as part of the 'Arab Spring'. It has also been dubbed the 'Facebook Revolution' because of the widespread use of social media platforms to communicate and assemble. Seen through the lens of the RP, this revolution can be interpreted as an event that happened before technology was prepared to fully support a progressive outcome. A revolution that arose in between the time when iconic leaders such as Lenin or Gandhi were necessary to represent people, and the revolutions of tomorrow where groups can successfully, peacefully, and legitimately harness the power of purpose-built software to enact change without a 'hero' or 'representative icon'.

SWITZERLAND: ANOMALY AT A TIME OF CRISIS

Our RP has had several anomalies. The god kings of ancient Egypt and Athenian democracy are historical examples, but it is the anomaly that we observe today at the time of paradigmatic crisis that is most relevant.

Switzerland is an outlier in its success according to modern economic and societal metrics as well as its quality of life and human average. This has largely been achieved due to its defiance of the RP and by being anomalous from two political perspectives. It is also anomalous for the longevity of its political stability, adherence to human rights, and equality among its citizens. These three anomalies make Switzerland an overall anomaly within the paradigm.

First, it is anomalous in that it is organised as what would be defined in the political language of RP1 as a direct democracy. It defies to a large extent the RP in that it has a markedly high level of representational equality. This is not to say that its distribution is fully equitable, but it is uniquely high. So while R≠1, R is high in relative paradigmatic terms.

Second, it is organised as a unique form of intergroup organisation. Swiss inter-cantonal and communal modes of interaction are uniquely well organised into a cohesive whole while respecting the individuality of each group. Groups of markedly different linguistic and cultural backgrounds have grouped to coexist with unique mechanisms of O.

Switzerland also has the distinction of not being a significant part of the crises of the Bridge. It is not part of the examples mentioned earlier in this chapter. It was not in the Second World War; it has no history of fascist rule or communist regime. It never properly joined the EU and is not a 'conventional' representative democracy. There have been no real revolutions nor periods of national psychosis because the people are more in charge than in other places.

Many excuses or explanations offered by non-Swiss people for its anomalous political organisation, representational equality, and success are made in conversation as well as academia. One regularly hears outrageous statements such as 'but they are so rich/educated/sensible/boring/lucky' or that 'their culture is different'. Swiss success and culture is a product and not the source of the mode of grouping, organisation, and equitable distribution of political representation. It is a federation. If all groups have the freedom to behave any way they like, they don't do so for long out of self-preservation. In the right structural context, they become forced to act in the common interest and progress.

This doesn't mean that Switzerland is without failings. There exists a class of citizens with unacceptably low levels of income who are disengaged from the political sphere. Furthermore, the cost of living is extremely high and Switzerland has a high per capita carbon footprint. Most of these failures (albeit failures by Swiss standards) can be interpreted as a result of being anomalous in terms of having a high R; despite this, they are still part of the paradigm in terms of the ideas they consider political. They still have left and right political parties and politicians that represent them. Political representation is not fully equitable and $R<1$.

The discussion about the Swiss anomaly does not imply that groups should follow the Swiss model or that it is the manifestation of a new paradigm. We are merely acknowledging a significant anomaly in a Kuhnian paradigm at a time of crisis. Furthermore, we are observing the positive consequences of semi-voluntary grouping and organisational modes that give higher levels of representational equality than others. Switzerland is the anomaly that hints at a potential new path towards another political paradigm without necessarily showing us what it should actually be.

END OF PHASE OR END OF PARADIGM?

And so it appears we are reaching the end of the Bridge. We stand at a time of significant paradigmatic crisis. One significant enough that it warrants discussion of the options to move into something new entirely. It also calls upon us to consider the consequences of merely enduring the coming changes and regression of our hard-won liberties. We may yet lose more than we have gained since the French Revolution in 1789. Only time will tell whether this statement is premature or if it has come too late. Whether we are already at the beginning of a new Orwellian, post-Bridge phase in our RP, or whether we will progress as a species into something new, remains to be seen.

A core obstacle to the arrival of a second RP is the baggage created by the thinkers of the Bridge, people like Rousseau and Marx. They have thought about the Bridge with one foot in the Absolutist phase by thinking on people's behalf. 'Bridgeism' as it were. We are still in the first phase with regard to the nature of the ideas that we consider political. Our current definition of what is political is bound by notions inherited from the Absolutist paradigm. In the way that Ptolemy was swept aside by Copernicus and that science has moved on from Aristotle, political thought is still partly stuck in 'Aristotelian mode'. We have grown out of his physics, medicine, and natural philosophy, but we are still very much his political descendants. We are still shackled. There are three important reasons why this is the case.

First, the Bridge is still young, we are barely 200 years out of the French Revolution. The Absolutist phase dominated for nearly 2,000 years. Technology is only starting to become capable of providing us with the tools for the final push either towards equality of R, or self-enslavement, or the complete destruction of civilisation, the latter two results ensuring that the Bridge is short-lived.

Second, we have mistakenly come to believe in political ideas in terms of their ability to provide solutions to humanity's problems. We have yet to fully move past this false hope, this 'belief' in a political idea. Political ideas that promise to provide answers and solve problems are holding us back and bringing out the worst in us.

Third, science, having had its Copernican moment, has the amazing ability to grow from paradigm to paradigm and contribute to humanity's experience at a greater and greater rate, enabling us to have better health, less hunger, and a myriad other wonders. Yet, what this has meant is that it has allowed us to endure our political folly. Our attachment of belief to political ideas: one of humanity's great self-delusions.

Political ideas and beliefs as we know them today could one day be to politics what alchemy now is to chemistry, astrology to astrophysics, and Galenism to anatomy once we shift properly into the second RP. A new era for humanity. An era of equality of R. Bridgeism has focused on ideas and not mechanisms, and so it comes with its baggage and we must work to shed it. In crude comparative terms, if Reagan exemplified the paradigmatic equivalent of Louis XIV, the 'high note' (neutral connotation) of a phase, the political leaders of the second decade of the 21st century could be the Louis XVIs, in relative paradigmatic terms. But humanity must make it so if it wants to evolve. It will not happen by itself. The beauty of this opportunity is that, in many places, revolution can happen peacefully and legitimately via vote.

Dangers of the Bridge

Only among the sciences is there true progress.

Isaac Asimov, cited in *A History of Mathematics**

The Bridge is a transition phase and, as with most structural transitions, it is fraught with instability and danger. The main danger to be addressed in this chapter is that we 'do' modern science and create modern technologies in antiquated socio-political contexts within which we frame 'modern political ideas'. We build the future living in an outdated structure where the framework and nature of the societies into which new technologies are born accentuate their problematic facets. Think, for example, of our changing view of social media. There is a rupture between the progress of science, its products, and politics in the sense that one has proceeded to develop exponentially while the other stagnates and benefits only from occasional incremental advancement. This is not entirely new and has been going on for quite some time. Starting with the industrial revolution of the 19th century, it has only become a potentially existential problem since

* Merzbach and Boyer, *A History of Mathematics* (Wiley, 2011) p. xi

the mid-20th century. The dangers we face as a species at the end of the Bridge are indicators of both a crisis in the Kuhnian sense as well as developments that present genuine existential threats to our species in its entirety. These dangers can be categorised under three main headings. First, there are existing, established technologies such as nuclear power and 'control technologies'. Second, we have technologies that are either on the cusp of becoming widely implemented or are anticipated to be widespread soon. These include artificial intelligence (AI), robotics, and genetic engineering. Third, we have sociopolitical contexts impeding the resolution of global issues such as climate change and communicable diseases. It must be said that these are things that force us to reconsider our relationship to the political and the structure of human interaction.

ESTABLISHED TECHNOLOGIES – NUCLEAR POWER

The harnessing of nuclear energy and its subsequent use in war is a prime example of the importance of the sociopolitical context in scientific development. There are over 25,000 nuclear weapons stockpiled by nation-states across the globe and only a small proportion of these would be needed to wipe us out entirely. Not only do we have enough weaponry to render ourselves extinct, but only a very small percentage of these weapons would be needed to cause irreparable damage to our societies of the kind from which it would take hundreds of years to recover. Nuclear technology has mostly been harnessed for war and destruction while the generation of the power angle has been mismanaged, remains controversial, and has taken a back seat.

Under different circumstances, it is possible that the word 'nuclear' would not necessarily have been associated with death and destruction and instead has come to signify electrical power. Los Alamos could have stayed a dusty, sleepy place and never have had anything to do with bombs. Physicist Freeman Dyson hoped that the processes started by the nuclear treaties of the 1970s and 1980s would be capable of leading to an era where 'gradually, as the decades of the 21st century roll by [...] the time may come when nuclear weapons are perceived as useless weapons of a vanished era [...] regarded as absurd and irrelevant, the time may come when it will be possible to get rid of them altogether'.* Several decades later, despite the potential of steps taken by our predecessors, such a day seems rather far off or even impossible. This is most pronounced when we consider the trajectory of powers such as Iran and North Korea in the late 2010s as well as superpowers' willingness to discuss the use of their own nuclear weapons as a viable military option. The current 'rogue nations' will also not be the last actors to seek access to such technologies.

CONTROL TECHNOLOGIES

The danger of scientific advancement without structural political evolution is not just about waiting for us to wipe ourselves out. It is also about political and social control. Technologies exist and are already in use by both governments and corporations that limit and control the extent of our

---

* Freeman Dyson, *The Scientist as Rebel* (NYRB, 2006) p. 130

freedoms or the access to information and tools that enable the exercise of liberty.

In dictatorships and pseudo-democracies across the globe, governments are increasingly adopting technologies that stifle not only dissent and protest but many other aspects of social and private life. This is done by securitising political interactions as well as those considered totally apolitical and mundane elsewhere. The term 'national security' is regularly adopted as a blanket term for political and social control. While these attitudes and practices are not new and the tyrant's desire to crush their opponents is a historical norm, the surveillance and violence meted out that was once reserved for political classes, factions, and rebel traitors (usually themselves aspiring tyrants) is now spreading to the control of entire populations. The example of a strictly regulated national Internet is a spreading norm among states who are increasingly finding access to tools to replicate restrictive environments for their citizens.

In Western representative democracies, the problems are in many ways more subtle. In several places, the ongoing collection of personal data by both state and companies makes many citizens uncomfortable. Generally, the use of this data, as well as the definition of what falls under the umbrella of national security, is defined by law, and there are specific procedures that ensure that such tools are not used for political or social ends. The concern here does not lie around the occasional and sometimes frequent illegal abuse (which is of course a genuine problem) of such systems but rather that the increase in surveillance and reduction in privacy can lead to the normalisation of practices that gradually lead towards control. Laws that protect liberties such as freedom of speech can be changed and do so regularly.

The extent to which these changes constitute a dangerous long-term trend remains the subject of debate. The West has seen elections in the last century which brought to power people who fortunately did not have access to today's data and technological tools. The possibility of similar choices of representatives from either the extreme right or left ends of the political spectrum is not something to be ruled out over a sufficiently long timeframe.

Nonetheless, concerns around control technologies are not just about dramatic repression by dictators (both elected and unelected) but also about an eventual return to slavery in a subtle new form and the end of the individual's freedom and liberty. It is not just concern about a controlled Internet (most readers may be actually unaware of what that looks and feels like because it's hard to imagine until you exist within it) but also the violence that befalls those who 'stray' and are therefore a threat. Will we see the point of no return before it's too late? It is highly plausible that we have already passed it and that standard forms of advocacy will not work to roll back the trend. There may indeed be no specific moment where control technologies become dangerous as new generations become acclimatised to systems their forebears would have found disturbing. The need for change in the fundamental structure of our sociopolitical systems has never been so pressing.

GENETIC ENGINEERING

There are scenarios, among many others, where developments in genetics could be used as an extension of control technologies. It is not hard to imagine a future regime enforcing 'foetus adjustments' to give birth to a generation of docile, domesticated, and compliant 'citizens' under the guise of fighting crime. Or, alternatively, the development of a class of humans with a more advanced genetic makeup at the expense of other sections of a group. Eugenics may indeed be an implausible prospect for Western democracies today, but most of the world's population do not live in such environments and many representative democracies are seeing the gradual erosion of their structures and face uncertain long-term futures where access to such technologies will be commonplace by then.

ROBOTICS

Developments in robotics in the early 21st century present one of the clearest examples of the fine line between a product of technology and science providing both immense advantages and danger to humans. Automation brings with it not only the promise of increased efficiency and profits for large corporations but also the replacement of dangerous, repetitive, or even sometimes menial functions previously executed by humans. While this may be aesthetically and financially appealing to C-suite executives who sit in offices far removed from the working conditions of their subordinates, it is problematic because these functions are currently indispensable sources of income for millions of people. Most of these functions do not pay well. Whether robotics is a danger to livelihoods or an opportunity to be seized as we create new jobs that provide higher incomes will depend on how things are approached as well as the rate of automation. The potential for social and political unrest as well as sudden widespread poverty for large segments of the world population is very serious.

Another dimension to the development of robotics is its potential application for war and violence against civilian populations. While the idea of not having to send humans to fight wars presents us with genuine opportunities to save lives, the application of robotics to machine and automated warfare depends almost entirely on the sociopolitical contexts within which the developments occur. The existence of inter-state warfare is a product of the existence of nation-states in the first place. As with any technology, robotics also has potential implications for control technologies.

ARTIFICIAL INTELLIGENCE

Artificial intelligence has been hailed both as humanity's antidote to all problems as well as the catalyst for the end of the human race. There exists a broad spectrum of views on the value, dangers, and opportunities of the widespread adoption of AI as well as the development of machines that surpass the human intellect. Similar to robotics, the role of AI in automation is poised to become significant, with sociopolitical benefits and effects depending on many factors.

The more alarming of the concerns regarding the arrival of AI are the implications for several 'control scenarios' where AI developments are used for population control. Whether this is through rethinking policymaking or what it means to survey and police law-abiding citizens, there are different scenarios where AI can either be controlled by nation-states or companies, or works of its own accord. Furthermore, we have also been warned of scenarios where AI wipes out or enslaves humanity entirely, again either under the guise of an evil corporation, a caricature of the bumbling scientist, or even of its own volition. The amount of speculation, as well as the extent of disagreement among experts, is astounding. Like many of the technologies discussed, the sociopolitical context into which the technology is born may be key.

There is also an increasing level of unease about the possibility of a future combination of AI and synthetic lifeforms (or even robotics) developing into a distinct and 'superior race' of non-human 'super-humans'. This hypothesis (not to be ruled out entirely on speculative grounds when one takes the long-term view) poses the genuinely old-school political question of 'what happens when new classes arise within a society?' with a new twist. The concept that the pre-existing stratification of human societies (hierarchies of social classes, ranks, and privilege) could, sickening as they already are, become even more complex and problematic with an added 'superior' non-human layer suggesting a reframing of the meaning of self in a humanity-crushing direction directly at odds with many existing values.

A brighter future may lie in the meagre hope that, should we manage to eliminate the concept of political hierarchy before such beings come to exist, they will, as products of their environment and 'us', fit into the flat hierarchies that humanity develops without too much damage. While this may appear to be a naive and simplistic argument, changing ourselves in advance may be the only hope we have. We have observed hierarchy in the animal kingdom but it is humanity that has developed it into something truly twisted. Hierarchy of course occurs naturally and is to be found everywhere from ants to wolves to people. However, it is specifically this fact that allows us to hope that artificial lifeforms, as opposed to those that have evolved from the animal kingdom, will not have a predisposition for power games unless we allow them (as we almost undoubtedly will to our own peril) to exist in a world where they find such structures to be a matter of fact and not a historical state of affairs. The beings it finds (us) to coexist with must be worthy of coexistence and much of that may depend on how we treat each other and our self-perception as a species when the day our first true 'other' observes and learns from and about us.

SCIENCE CONSTRAINED: CLIMATE CHANGE

The onset of manmade climate change is perhaps the most dangerous single trend or event ever faced by humanity. Ironically, despite all the horrible things humans have done to each other, this crisis is not (while admittedly caused by us) a directly human-to-human threat. Its potential consequences could reshape our existence and relationship to the planet and each other. It could be the destroyer of human civilisation, making politics and its paradigms appear petty in their narrow focus on humanity. It also places our current Representational Paradigm (RP) in need of urgent attention because it is the future of life itself on the planet that we imperil, not just our material well-being. We must find mechanisms of legislation that allow us to act where our representatives have failed.

The emergence of increasing levels of public awareness and anger at the inaction of representatives is perhaps best noticed by the emergence of generational icons such as Greta Thunberg. As frustration mounts, the need for citizens to have a direct say in environmental policy is an increasingly appealing path to implementing solutions which lie in existing and proven technologies but whose adoption is impeded by sociopolitical contexts. Fossil fuel profits and political interests, as well as sociocultural baggage, stand in the way of solving what is potentially one of the most damaging long-term planetary crises. Swapping out legacy systems is never completely smooth and yet we have no choice.

SCIENCE CONSTRAINED: HEALTH AND DISEASE

Another important aspect of human development that could save lives and improve the quality of life for billions is the attempt to eradicate communicable diseases.

Examples such as the effort against polio have proven that the goals are achievable but remain elusive due to social norms, local politics, and the interference of national governments. The campaign by the Gates Foundation was met with significant resistance in both Afghanistan and Pakistan for precisely those reasons, making them the last remaining hiding places from whence polio may spring back. Polio could have been fully eradicated, setting a precedent in human history and a blueprint from which to work systematically against all communicable diseases.

This problem has become particularly pointed in light of the COVID-19 pandemic where representatives proved themselves generally incapable of coordinating and aligning in transparent and constructive ways across international borders. This does not mean that there have not been many people (including some representatives) who have not made the most commendable efforts, but rather it is an observation that our sociopolitical systems were not ready for something that many scientists and healthcare-policy professionals predicted would occur at some point. Many feel let down by the people they chose to represent them or by those who took it upon themselves to represent.

RE-SKILLING AND RE-CLAIMING

The next industrial revolution, as it has been called, in its early stages, has generated considerable anxiety and fear. The populism of the early 21st century is partially the result of advancing technological change, and questions humanity's role in a world where there are fewer 'jobs' (in the sense that we understand the term today). Eventually, a new *raison d'être* will be needed. The intensity of what is coming will require a rethinking of the reasons for our existence as much as our sources of income. But how to achieve a weekly wage or monthly salary in a world with more humans and less 'work'?

A possible approach could be a two-pronged strategy of 're-skilling and re-claiming'. Re-skilling is something for the transition period. This concept already exists in the form of government and other programmes; if scaled in the right way, re-skilling could mitigate some of the short- and medium-term effects of industrial automation.

Re-claiming, on the other hand, is more a fundamental and conceptual notion for the long term, one which may also need preparation and open discussion. In a world with less 'work', new options and directions must be found for humanity. One way of addressing this would be through 're-claiming' certain areas and fields from AI and technology before they are fully adopted. There is a need for collective agreement that some things are best kept for humans because they have been selected as our future occupations, sources of income, and providers of happiness on a much wider scale than they are today. There are major practical impediments to the answer to the question, 'what should we keep for ourselves?' Possibilities include games (especially digital ones) and their associated industries, sports, all of the arts, crafts (bringing back the idea that something handmade is special and has intrinsic value precisely because it is not made by a machine), childbearing and rearing, the care of animals, and other things. 'AI-made' paintings and music are still novel, but examples of machine learning and AI outplaying humans at games such as Go and Dota 2 are potentially more than demonstrations of prowess. They indicate the emergence of a broad group of things that need to be kept exclusively human centred if we are to have purpose as a species in the very long run.

None of this will be enough to fulfil and pay billions of people during any transition phase. What could be added to occupy us in a way that is fulfilling and pays is 'politics redefined'. Under the correct organisational and representational structure, the legislating and solving of public problems via larger groups of people could serve both as a block to the dangers of technologies mentioned above and a way to remunerate vast swathes of populations that work less and require a supplemented income.

SARAH CONNOR AS ALLEGORY

The character Sarah Connor in the *Terminator* movies came back to warn humanity of the impending AI robot takeover and the dangers of Skynet. These extreme scenarios, taken seriously by many experts, may serve as an allegorical warning. Indeed AI may one day be able to 'run' and manage our politics and other problem solving for us. But whether it is us who hands over or it 'takes over' is a key difference. Perception will be key to reception. A politics redefined and prepared for the 21st and 22nd centuries may eventually become more of a chore for many than the prize of a few. At that point, the sociopolitical context would allow us to happily hand over the responsibility to technology completely because problem solving of that type has by then become a menial burden; similar to having a washing machine for our laundry rather than doing it by hand. Going from representative democracies or even less equitable structures to AI-driven politics would be awful. We would be enslaved. But if we change the definition of what is political and relegate today to a bygone era, we may eventually get disinterested and bored. At that point, we could get technology to do it all for us because the idea will be born at the appropriate time and in the appropriate sociopolitical context. More importantly, those welcoming it would be different.

Technology is only technology because it is not yet completely pervasive. There is a word for it because it is still a thing. One day it will be us and will not have its own word. It will be meshed with our existence in a way that will make us unable to differentiate between what was once two distinct things. Who we are as this happens will define our future.

SOCIOPOLITICAL CONTEXT IS KEY

A core danger of the Bridge is that the scientific advancements of the age are too far ahead of the sociopolitical contexts in which they are being developed to be a safe and guaranteed positive contribution to society. It was bearable to have our existing sociopolitical contexts until we invented things like nuclear bombs. For science and technology to make their fullest positive contribution to the human experience, we need to provide sociopolitical contexts in which the paradigm allows for science to develop in a way which is more likely to be safe for humans.

Artificial intelligence, bio-tech, and other upcoming seismic changes should be born into societies where their dangers are of less concern because humanity has moved on from the structures, activities, and interactions which constitute dangerous behaviour. Contrary to the view of many, it is not these scientific advances that will free us of our sociopolitical context, but the opposite. These technological advances run the risk of either killing us all or enslaving us. Therefore, it is us who needs to change, to ensure that science will always be able to contribute a net good to all. Scientific progress in turn has given us many wondrous things and has allowed us to stagnate and accept the musical chairs we play on the canon of political and philosophical ideas. This structure appears to many to be increasingly outdated and yet progress in science and prosperity has allowed us to endure our own folly and not be forced to move into something truly new. It is precisely because the statistical trends that we have decided to use to define our success as a species (GDP, birth rates, life expectancy, etc.) have never been so good that we fail to look at the history of our ideas and assume, collectively, deludedly, that forward is better across disciplines. But politics is not mathematics, and the progress has not been linear. Moreover, unlike the natural sciences, you cannot comfortably claim that you are uncovering the 'truth' when you think of political ideas. We almost all agree that we are engaging with human constructs and yet somehow we treat them as if they are immovable because they are the sociohistorical products. That is why, in the early 21st century, fears and anxieties have propelled us towards a new phase of authoritarianism, populism, and the reinforcement of totalitarian ideas in new places as well as in states where that has always been the norm. All at a time when things have never been statistically better.

When one considers the amount of academic and scientific research, the number of books published that is ongoing today, one could argue that historically there weren't many ideas in terms of sheer volume. Tangentially this could suggest that the idea of 'canons', instead of being viewed as selective and restrictive reading on the history of ideas, could be seen as a summary of what was, in purely quantitative terms, not much thought. There has perhaps been more idea generation in the last hundred years than there has ever been in all of human history. While it is true that not much of this modern thought (especially political thought) has been paradigm breaking, our historical lack of options means that we have developed the reflex of latching onto political concepts with all our hopes, dreaming that we would be pulled forward and out of what can only be described by today's standards as general misery. It also means that we have never undertaken to fundamentally rethink what constitutes a political idea by reconsidering what we understand to be political.

Two thousand years ago, just as in the Middle Ages, ideas were all we had. But now we have science and it has taken over much of this role. Politics is in the way of development. What we have not realised is that while science and technological development has indeed bucked the trend and moved from alchemy to chemistry and astrology to astronomy on a long-term irreversible trajectory of progress, it is a false idol if we hope it will do for us in politics what is has done for us in health and comfort. It could mean our enslavement. We need to drop science as an idol for our politics and chart a parallel curve for politics which will allow us to genuinely evolve as a species.

The philosophy and history of science give scientists a very good idea of where they are coming from and where they are going. They are sure to go forward. This is because science progresses (I am speaking of the natural sciences). It took a lot of going round in circles before they broke free and moved forward, but it has been achieved and humanity has reaped the benefits. Nobody is about to rediscover that the Earth is actually flat or that Galileo deserved his miserable treatment. Basic mathematical concepts are not dismissed and re-embraced at generational intervals, yet it appears that politics and political philosophy cannot have that. The reason we believe this lie is because people tend to embrace one of two evils:

1. That an 'ism' or political belief is a solution instead of an ingredient. An answer to our lack of progress or the problems of the day or forever;
2. That, like science, politics needs no 'isms', no belief, and no 'thought'. That it can be treated as a science.

Despite what may seem to be much pessimism, there is hope for the future of our relationship with technology. Many fields such as healthcare and education are being enhanced and rethought, with amazing implications for the future. Nor is everything dark for the relationship between the political field (in the broad sense) and technology. There is always the hope that sociopolitical contexts will develop to give technology a new meaning or even vice versa. Blockchain is an example of a technology that suggests the possibilities for sociopolitical change despite the concerns that exist about its long-term viability and scalability. Despite such examples, the ball remains in the court of humanity for what is possibly our only window of opportunity to ensure that our relationship with technology becomes one of increasing freedoms and not the opposite.

Neither science nor politics alone could kill us. It is the increasing divergence in their level of progress and the implications of the sociopolitical context in which science and technology are developing that are the existential threat to humanity. Half-hearted attempts will not work; we need a new paradigm and we need to move quickly to provide healthy sociopolitical contexts for the arrival of technologies that will reshape and perhaps even end humanity.

ETUDE 1

Politics in a New Kuhnian Paradigm

If the only contribution of this book is that there is some consensus among readers that we should engage with political ideas from the viewpoint that we need a 'Copernican moment' then it has been successful. The history of both science and politics shows that the enemies of progress (the conservatives, reactionaries, and forces of darkness) are the default. It is the light which attacks them. Not them that attack the light. One reason why progress does not always win in politics is that we regularly lose sight of the fact that we are on the offensive, but rather think that it is about defence. Progress is, by nature, an aggressive attack on the entrenched. But worse than in science, political progress is held back by interests and haunted by beliefs inherited from our predecessors. From the Axis of Ancients, Aristotle still stands in politics, if only metaphorically. If we are to outgrow him and the other foundational political thinkers of the first Representational Paradigm (RP1) then politics must come to mean something entirely new. We need to shift away from our RP as the dangers of not doing so outweigh the temporary comforts of societies languishing in apathy.

We are searching for a point of departure. There needs to be a conscious search by many for the next paradigm. How we experiment and search for equitable and sustainable modes of political organisation will define the types of societies we live in once we rebuild. What must be new is that there must be equal effort from all because it is genuinely to everyone's benefit to pursue a future that ensures true equality. Instead of focusing on specific equalities, it is perhaps the meta-structure that needs rethinking, with equality being achieved as a consequence rather than as a (noble) goal. What is also important is that enough people engage with the need for a paradigm shift and agree to try out new things because: a) we are aware of the potential benefits (look at science's trajectory); and b) the current lack of paradigm shift is dangerous and untenable. As such, humanity must actively experiment to produce politics' Copernican moment, because otherwise we will keep rolling around in the quagmire in which we find ourselves, shifting from one monism to the next, incapable of achieving something that ensures genuine progress. The forces of relativism (the only morally safe 'ism' out there), are fundamentally weak unless protected by a new meta-frame. There has been no significant structural political progress in recent times and science has allowed us to endure our own backwardness. But for how long?

This is not a call for politics to become more 'scientific', but rather for us to find a way forward which allows us to emulate science's ability to progress from paradigm to paradigm, mindset to mindset, and age to age peacefully and without bloodshed and barbarism. For a field other than the sciences to consistently provide positive products for humanity.

Nietzsche, in his *On the Genealogy of Morality*,* taught us that existing concrete, ethical systems have been developed by a sociohistorical process and that today we have to formulate

* Friedrich Nietzsche, *On the Genealogy of Morality* (CUP, 2017)

'on Earth', as opposed to 'from heaven' or prescribed elsewhere, discriminating solutions for difficult problems especially in relation to morality. In the political world, we need to break from the notion that politics should be a reflection of a personal or public morality or even of history. We must do this so that each of us can, individually and together, help ourselves as a species to become what we could be. A unique problem-solving group in charge of it is destiny. That we may one day look at ourselves in the mirror and at our past and exclaim, 'Behold the humans! We have come far since our suffering'.

RESHAPING REPRESENTATION

The following section uses the argument that Representation (R) and its nature form a Kuhnian paradigm as a point of departure; a primordial paradigm that has existed since we have grouped. It started, proverbially, as soon as a third person joined Adam and Eve, giving birth to the political. We are here to change the meaning of politics by bringing it back to its fundamentals and evolving forwards in a direction that is chosen, as opposed to inherited or imposed. We must, therefore, begin by returning to our definition of 'politics devoid of paradigm' to find a new path to tread:

> Politics is the nature of human interactions that occur when humans group.

From this, we see that rather than a concrete thing, politics is an essence that permeates the fabric of our lives. Only from here can we build anew. We live in a paradigm in which we are represented by others and this contextualises our political existence and has a deep interconnection with the organisational strand of politics. Why leave the paradigm? Because it no longer works for us, but where are we to move to as the house crumbles? We are both unfortunate and blessed to live at the end of politics' first real Kuhnian paradigm. Unfortunate because ends can be ugly, blessed because we may yet live to glimpse the beauty of a chosen destiny in a Kuhnian paradigm of our choosing.

What characteristics of R do we aspire to? R=1, nothing less. That is the hallmark of the new paradigm. Equality of R through self-representation in legislation and other areas of the political. But it must start with equality of R in legislation and changes to the fundamental nature of our relationship with how the law is made. Only from there might we become truly equal. We must represent ourselves and cut out the landlord posing as the middleman. We must own and choose our laws, our futures, and our common destiny. We must seek genuine representational equality for the first time ever because it will enable us to provide sociopolitical contexts within which humanity can truly thrive and fix problems that have hitherto remained unresolved. Other types of equality among human beings will stem from that as well as the harnessing of technology to provide globally available mechanisms of governance as a core functional component of a politics redefined.

What would that change in practical terms? It could change everything. Most importantly, changing the nature of R and moving it to 1 triggers a genuine opportunity to reshape our sociopolitical systems into something built instead of inherited and suffered. How we group, how we interact, and how groups interact can and must be rethought. We would have a unique opportunity to rethink the structure of things so that we can all benefit and interact healthily. Changing R is the easiest way to reshape the organisational strand of politics and truly change its meaning. We could heal our end-of-paradigm ailments and face the future with a new toolkit. So much is resolved at the beginning of new paradigms. The vitality of a new lens and the wonder of new tools to solve both old and new problems. But what does this actually mean? And is it really change?

DIRECTORSHIP

We have mentioned the fact that in a new Kuhnian paradigm, specifically one where the nature of R is what we change (where R=1), politics might gain an entirely new meaning. Today most of us are citizens but there are some who are not even that and have been failed miserably. Perhaps our understanding of citizenship as a concept, whether we are representatives or not, is something that can be evolved out of, by virtue of a new Kuhnian paradigm. By this we mean moving from citizenship to Directorship. Citizens becoming Directors.

> By citizen we mean the person of the Bridge, the humans we see today, with their corresponding rights and responsibilities. Their sense of self, beliefs, and ideas. All existing within the structure of the Bridge and RP1.
>
> By Director we mean the person of tomorrow, the humans we could become, with their corresponding rights and responsibilities. Their sense of self, beliefs and ideas. All existing within the structure of a new Kuhnian paradigm: the paradigm of Directorship.
>
> In RP2, R=1.
>
> In RP2 there are no citizens, just Directors.

A Director is a lawmaker.

A Director is a legislator.

We are all Directors in our new paradigm.

A Director is any adult human, born of any creed, nation, race, gender, class, or other Bridgeist notion, who has the rights and bears the responsibilities of what was once reserved for representatives.

A Director takes the time needed to apply themselves to their new vocation and is compensated fairly.

There is no exclusivity, being an adult human is the sole criteria for eligibility.

Being human is enough for us to qualify. We know what we are and can come to be only if we make it so.

As we enter a new Kuhnian paradigm, Directorship has three core components. These are not everything, but a start to something:

1. Direct Representation
2. Means as Ends
3. Temporal Relativism

The first is the toolkit we use.

The second is a lens to help us refocus.

The third, a door to walk through.

DIRECT REPRESENTATION

The only mechanism of self-representation is Direct Representation (DR). By this, we mean the direct and equal 'say' or 'vote' of individuals on all matters of legislation, governance, and/or other areas of public life that are selected to be democratised.

How and what we govern in a system of DR will be affected by our political choices which will define which individuals vote for what, who can and cannot vote, and how groups interact, as well as many other things. The basic principle of R is simple. People will represent themselves and contribute equally and fully to political decision-making as a part-time vocation, and we will be paid for our time and effort. In a way, it will become something that we all share and do in common. We will do it ourselves because the kings, dictators, aristocrats, demagogues, and representatives have, for the most part, failed us. The Bridge was about clawing back R, but it is dying and its fruits are rotting. It could not make it to the end of the road and set us truly free. We will have to take ourselves there.

Direct Representation is a mechanism. It holds no bias, is not born of Bridgeist Political Belief (BPB), and holds no promise of a solution. It is the cornerstone of a political meta-frame that rather than promising a solution, empowers us to take responsibility and resolve issues. This is what makes it something to fear in the Bridge and a tool of hope for the Directors of Directorship. What something means depends on the context within which the question is framed. What we do with our tools depends on who we are when we use them. We seek equal and full participation by all and will accept nothing less because we are worth more. Direct Representation is the product of a decision to create equal R. It is also a form of direct responsibility and from there, growth and progress.

In the Bridge, DR may sound like a dangerous tyranny of the majority. In the Bridge, such a majority would be guided by the fury of an entire paradigm's worth of legitimate grievances as well as unshaken ideological baggage (BPB). However, we are not suggesting DR is implemented in the Bridge. Rather we are going to implement it to bring about the Bridge's end. It is at first a catalyst and later a mechanism. Direct Representation for the people of the Bridge is an Armageddon, but for Directors it could be a tool of destiny, precisely because being a Director is a new existence, not just a change in R.

The prism of seeing our decisions as delegated to representatives has reduced our ownership and appreciation of the genuine effects, whether positive or negative, of our collective decisions, allowing us to make the same mistakes and revolve around similar ideas time and time again. Some problematic political concepts have been with us from the very beginning and still haunt us. People only represent others (have to/claim to) because there is underrepresentation in the first place. It is like fixing an unacknowledged problem with a doomed solution. In some places with higher R, we have come to believe that fairness in the selection of representatives is democracy itself and that its values can be relinquished. What that really amounts to is the use of democratic means to appoint people whose function is, in today's world, anti-democratic.

Direct Representation is not itself our entire framework. It is a tool that when used within Directorship becomes part of a mechanism of inclusion and equality. It is not a solution but a method to choose solutions. It is also not an idea in the Bridgeist sense of the term, but only a way. We need a framework that can evolve out of Bridgeist belief, and DR is only a part of that. The product we seek is a politics redefined. The fact that politics defines us at all is a consequence of the nature we have ascribed to it. We have defined it as such: a controller of humanity. It is precisely because it is a human construct and not a natural phenomenon that we can reconstruct it from the ground up so that we can define it and maintain control over that definition.

How will we know when we have entered the new paradigm? When R=1. When the distribution of political representation is equal for all. Call it power, call it voice, call it contribution. It must be equal. When it forms the fundamental metric of equality from which others may spring forth and the equalities we (legitimately) worry about today fall into place as a consequence instead of being goals to achieve. Here we enter the unknown empowered, facing the future armed with the tools of legislation and democratised decision-making. We seek to harness the power of choice.

Technology today is, as it was for the scientific revolution, the prime mover and we hold the tools for our emancipation in our hands (perhaps even literally via our phones). The interconnectedness available to us through the Internet must come to be a positive product of technology. So far it has shown it comes with many dangers. How we use a technology says so much about the beings we are and, in turn, certain facets of our humanity are accentuated, both negative and positive. It is because Directorship is essentially a natural mechanism of empowerment that it is made accessible via modern methods as both are enabling mechanisms. Interconnectedness means that ideas collide that would never have done so, in ways that could not have been previously imagined. We must turn these tools and make them work for humanity instead of letting them bring out our negative facets. We seek a single level for the legislative. A level that includes all voices and where they are heard. One of the first things we must come to realise is that politics should not provide answers and solutions but be a conduit for decision-making and a mechanism for solving problems. Our relationship to the word must change and, as such, we must change its meaning.

Copernicus' model was a major change for astronomy in the sense that it put the sun at the centre of the universe, as opposed to the Earth. This meant that the planets fell into logical sequence. It was something new and incredible to many at the time, but today is seen as completely normal. A new perspective just by reordering and rethinking. The change we seek through Directorship is about putting the individual at the centre of our conceptual universe. The individual is an idea that will become what we make of it and we must rethink the age-old notion of balance between individual and community by rethinking the idea of collective and community. We must all work to produce that Copernican moment in politics. We are in RP1 and its language defines politics. When we evolve out of RP1, we will change the meaning of politics and humanity in turn.

As Directors we may seek to break walls and borders as a consequence, not a goal. Globalism as a consequence of individual representation as opposed to globalism as a goal. Unless of course Directors decide to not make it a goal. In general, we need ideas that we share that define us all beyond the Bridgeist conception of 'nation', 'race', 'religion', or other exclusive and exclusionary grouping methods learnt in RP1. If it is true that humankind has enough similarities to allow us to grow past our differences, if given the right context, then this will eventually be reflected in a global Directorship. If it is not true, then we must at least use our new paradigm to create methods of intergroup interaction that are healthy, tenable, and non-confrontational, perhaps by expanding the Swiss idea of the canton in tangential directions.

As Directors we are seeking for entire populations to gain these rights and responsibilities through legitimate, peaceful means and, in turn, change the nature and role of state and law. The nation-state as we know it increased R historically but now reduces it and so it must go, but in a way both defined and guided by us because we have developed a new sense of what we seek. A positive process, not a knee-jerk reaction, via the political self-determination for the individual.

There are other options for humanity other than a new Kuhnian paradigm for R. We could decide not to act and have our hard-earned gains of R reduced; snatched from our grasp by companies, groups, states, and other powers. All with the technologies we could use to free ourselves. We could even do away with R altogether and hand everything over to an algorithm and add new depth to our experience of subservience and docility, putting humanity on its knees and making us worse off than at the beginning of the paradigm where Pharaohs ruled with godlike power. The option is there waiting for us at the crossroads should we prefer to select the easier route.

It may be historically unique that we have an opportunity at this specific juncture to really reconsider things. This is perhaps the moment for the unleashing of our human potential, to choose what we leave behind, what we take with us, and what we can build that is new. We could rethink our relationship with politics, its ideas, and what it means for an idea to be political in the first place. We could reshape the meaning of politics itself by choosing to leave the Bridge for a world of R=1. The COVID-19 pandemic and the response of many of our representatives and sociopolitical systems has highlighted the flaws of the Bridge to the point where we are no longer able to deny them.

We have discussed a toolkit to use. Let us move on and discuss our problematic relationship with two interconnected words: 'Means' and 'Ends'.

MEANS AS ENDS

Topias (Places)

Let us be clear. I do not speak of utopia. Directorship is not about finding a utopia. Nor do I seek to appropriate the word by diluting its meaning and using it to discuss what is possible. Utopias are imaginary worlds where we, as humans filled with both hope and despair, seek to imagine a better existence that we know cannot be. We devour utopias in the books we read, the visual media we absorb, and the art we create.

The word utopia comes from the Greek for 'nowhere' or 'no-place',* because utopia does not exist. By definition, utopias are 'expressions of desire'† acknowledged as mere fancies, but they are also expressions of something much deeper and are a recurrent theme across time and place. They underline the fact that we are fundamentally dissatisfied with our lot. They are the dreams of people neither in charge nor in control. The dreams of people no longer living in a Hobbesian 'state of nature' and yet who behave as if change isn't on the horizon and, in material terms, is generally already here. The dreams of an inherited subservient mentality. Other types of utopia are those we believe to be real despite not having seen them for ourselves. The multiple historical incarnations of the 'Kingdom of Heaven' across cultures are perhaps the most extreme expressions of our hope and despair and the outcome of a desire to make utopias 'real'. With the ultimate abandonment of hope of the possibility of changing how we live and who we are, they have been used as a carrot and

---

* John Carey, ed. *The Faber Book of Utopias* (Faber and Faber, 1999) p. xi

† Ibid., n.d.

stick to get us to 'behave' in the face of the prospect of technological and cultural stasis. Whatever does not grow must decay and so we have sought to 'whip' things and people to keep them in 'shape'. Progress could be so much more for a world that has moved on from the mirage of fixed dogma and welcomes the tools of legislation as something owned and held in common.

Today we do not live in a utopia. We live in 'ontopia', the place that 'is'. We live in reality, in the here and now. Directorship seeks to change one thing about ontopia: the nature of R. To end a paradigm. But what is important is who we are as we enter a chapter of equality of R. I do not speak of the 'U-human', someone from a utopia, because they have a mind that cannot exist; we do not have the foresight to imagine them to make them real, nor should we accept the 'O-human', the person of today, because of their suffering. The O-human is programmed by their context to be either ruler or ruled where both are slaves to their paradigm. We are looking to change ourselves as part of the end of the paradigm. This book is as much about finding the 'Ei-human' (or the 'person that could be': the future Director), as it is about embracing a new 'self' as we move forward and evolve. It is only then that 'eitopia', or the world that can be, comes into existence. Eitopia becomes our new ontopia when we embrace the possibilities that we allow ourselves by entering a new Kuhnian paradigm. When we first change ourselves, perhaps only then will we truly rebuild the world in our new image. It must all start by moving R to 1.

All cultures (at least all those of the first RP) have imagined utopias in some shape or form and will continue to do so. Directors don't dream of utopia. Utopias are portrayals of outcomes, a kind of snapshot, whereas Directorship is about process and from there, progress. Mechanisms and not solutions. Means and not ends. Directors mould their societies and fashion the world as they desire it to be like clay in the hands of a sculptor. That is also why I will not present an image of how I wish the world to be 'after' we grow into Directorship, lest those who keep their slave mentality use it to daydream. I will keep my views to the value of one vote, because if we can progress into another paradigm and learn to evolve and grow, then means are what matters because there will be no end.

The Human Mean

The 'human average' is a concept that spouts more from an analysis of peoples' state of mind; intellectual and cognitive development as opposed to traditional economic and 'prosperity' metrics. From a historical perspective, our average human has improved significantly over time. We are reaching a phase in our development where we could make a conscious decision to accelerate the average human within a generation instead of more. The point on the curve where we could shoot up, propelled by compounded knowledge, literacy rates, and the technology to reach and teach people in even the remotest corners of the Earth.

Reading one hundred works can get you through the canons of both Greece and Rome. If 99% of what was written was lost to the sands of time, then that takes us to a mere 10,000 works. Icelanders say that there is at least one book in each of us (and by 'us' they mean themselves). There are approximately 345,000 living Icelanders right now at this moment. This gives a sense of the scale of the development the people of such a nation have undergone.

The transformation that the world has undergone must be sped up, because we are neither so ignorant that we can be 'managed' the way we once were, nor have we reached the point where we govern ourselves. Imagining a new human average for ourselves, with its image ever evolving, helps us conceptualise the future towards which we are working as the lawmakers of tomorrow. Another word for average is 'mean'. The human mean.

Politics as Perfecting Means

A Poem

They said the ends justify the means
Those princes of old
And the reps follow suit

Means to ends
End of freedom
With ends in sight
Us in their sights

From there the mean human
With a lowered mean
Living a life so mean
But what is it that we mean?

We mean that our mean
Is not as mean as it may seem
Indeed the mean has risen
Despite princes so mean

We seek to mean
Something different:
A new human mean

Born of a shared dream
Of means as ends
Not perfect ends

Just perfecting means
Raising the mean
That is what we see

The rise of means
Humanity without end or ends
Bury the three

The Axis Ancient
The Old Bridge
The Florentine Prince

That my prince is your mirror
That you may rise
And look upon yourself
And see nothing mean
But rather arise
Eight billion, princely

TEMPORAL RELATIVISM

> The value of a Bridgeist Political Belief is relative to its practical usefulness at the time of asking and nothing more.

Ever strive for the whole; and if no whole thou canst make thee,
Join, then, thyself to some whole, as a subservient limb!

A Poet of the Bridge*

PRODUCTS OF THE BRIDGE

Political beliefs and modern political thought are products of our paradigm and the Bridge. They are products of the modes of grouping and organisation that humans have pursued since the end of Absolutism and the divine right of kings into the beginning of the 21st century.

There have been many different and diverse political ideas espoused in what is, in historical terms, a relatively short period and when one takes the broadest paradigmatic view, all are part of the same chapter in our thought. Most of these ideas share two defining factors. First, political ideas tend to be constructed as belief systems and are presented as either solution providers or solutions in and of themselves. Alternatively, they espouse ideals that lead to conclusions about a fixed notion of how a society 'should' or 'could' be. This leftover from Absolutism continues to play a significant

* Friedrich Schiller, "The Duty of All" in *The Poems of Schiller,* trans. E. Bowring, eds. Ann C. Weaver, Martin Swales, and Matthew Bell (George Bell, 1893)

role in informing many political ideas as well as how people engage with them. Second (and here the fault is ours), humanity has generally responded by believing in political ideas and their ability to provide answers to questions and solutions to problems. Most of us tend to believe in political ideas to some degree or another and are drawn to them. Despite all of this, they can be viewed as transient and a symptom of our current paradigm where there is neither political representation nor genuine equality of R. And so we mistakenly look to politics, its thinkers, and their ideas for answers and solutions.

The Bridge has not led us to be truly free because it did not go far enough. The nature of modern political belief as a product of the Bridge has been alluded to as having caused much of today's political quagmire. But how then do we look at political belief and assess whether there really is a problem and need for a fundamental change in our relationship with it?

PARADIGM CONTENDERS

The history of political thought can be thought of as largely being defined by 'paradigm contenders'. Ideas that aspire to impose themselves as Kuhnian paradigms by virtue of their structure and content. Examples include socialism, fascism, liberalism, and communism. None of these has managed to become a globally dominant paradigm in their heated tussle for the exclusion of the others. The Bridge is full of these contenders because the structure of our sociopolitical systems and the nature of political belief today lends itself to ideas that want to dominate. This is in part because they are designed to do so and that is why they contend. These ideas present themselves as 'truths' or the embodiments of truths such as those 'felt'. They are transparent constructs of products of sociohistorical forces and yet they are regularly presented or at least engaged with as if they embody 'truths' that even scientific observations don't enjoy after passing peer review.

WHY DO WE BELIEVE IN POLITICAL IDEAS?

There are many theories and reasons explaining belief in both individuals and groups. Some of these have emerged from the field of neuroscience, others from the social sciences, or humanities, or elsewhere. Here, we focus on a specific set of reasons for political belief. This is neither an attempt to actively exclude or replace other theories, nor to deny or endorse them, but rather focus on a specific aspect of our problematic relationship with belief itself.

Belief attempts to fulfil the same fundamental human need as grouping and organisation, both of which are a product of primal instinct: they are about survival. The need to survive creates the need to feel safe, which has led to the desire to belong to groups. From there we come to believe in ideas shared by these groups or identities to which we belong or wish to belong.

Seen in reverse, political belief is in part a direct product of the need to belong, which most people feel naturally in some shape or form, whether consciously or subconsciously. From sports teams to political parties or religion, people are naturally attracted to groups, partly from the need to feel safe.

Being part of a group makes us feel safer because it increases our chances of survival, which is a primal instinct.

Hence political grouping and organisation. Belief and politics are thus intertwined not because they are fundamentally interrelated, but because they are two things humans continually do in order to increase their chances of survival. Their interconnection may be more the result of the historical process of us linking them than their fundamental nature. The extreme Bridgeist example of this is when people group because of a shared political belief, leading to the creation of political parties.

Even in the act of rejecting the views of a group, we align with another and only very rarely find ourselves alone. It is we who intertwine two separate things to increase our chances of survival and this is sometimes subconscious in that we do not necessarily need to feel it for it to happen. We can also feel 'convinced' by what we believe is correct or some sort of truth at the most rational of levels. This is an important reason for why we absorb incorrect or thoughtless information and values as received from a source, at times regardless of veracity, especially when linked to our problematic relationship with authority and authoritative sources.

These are human tendencies that have permeated the political language of both the Absolutist and Bridge phases of the paradigm but which have increasingly frustrated peoples as time has progressed and the human average has improved. Humans have tended to group naturally around authority and very few political groups consciously engage and wrestle with the conceptual notion of the act of grouping before they do so, applying Bridgeist structures and modes of thought as a natural consequence of the context within which they are formed.

Does a human, forever alone in the wilderness, born alone and destined never to meet another human, believe?

Do they believe naturally without influence or grouping? If this person does not believe naturally, then it begs the question as to whether belief is a consequence of grouping. Or, on the other hand, perhaps it is belief that is a natural occurrence that happens anyway in the human condition, in which case it happens when we group (or interact with one) because both happen all the time. Thus, we might be linking two separate things. We can believe in something shared by no one else, even a political idea. Belief distinct from grouping exists independently. People can also group without belief.

Can there be humanity without belief or grouping? Aristotle tells us that 'he who is unable to live in society, or who has no need because he is sufficient for himself, must be either beast or god'.* Could it be that we are somehow both, with the latter suppressed by our modes of grouping and our politics? There is no humanity without grouping and yet we tend to do it politically without giving it the degree of reflection it deserves. We may think deeply about political questions, and yet the acts of grouping and organising are not things that have been revised to maximum benefit.

Belief, in general, is also a valuable cornerstone of our existence. It is belief that prevents us from falling into the abyss of nihilism. If we could fulfil the need to guarantee the survival of our species by changing our sociopolitical contexts, then maybe we could let go of the other; not necessarily the need to believe in and of itself but the need to believe in political ideas. What if we could group in ways

* Aristotle, *The Politics and the Constitution of Athens*, ed. Stephen Everson (CUP, 1996)

which would allow us to not need 'modern' political beliefs because we have found modes of grouping and organisation that ensure survival and give societies tools to solve problems without entangling fear, power, despair, and hope? Directorship could do that but only if our minds are open to the breadth of possibilities of an entirely new Kuhnian paradigm.

POLITICAL BELIEF TODAY

The application of value-based solutions to practical issues has demonstrated itself to be dangerous and central to many of the modern problems of the Bridge. This is because of the current nature of our belief in political ideas and the fact that there is belief 'in' politics. There have also been attempts at the total removal of values from politics. One of the reasons these attempts have failed to remove them from the structure of political interaction is the current nature of R. In our RP, a group is represented by a representative, who regularly claims to reflect values as part of their appeal. If the nature of political ideas changes by virtue of entering a new paradigm, then we will no longer need to believe in political ideas like we used to, and so belief and politics could become unrelated categories. The structure of a core facet of our existence could be reshaped; but is that desirable or even possible? Considering the crisis of our paradigm, it is at least necessary to stop believing in the Bridgeist ideal of political belief as the solution. But how then do we proceed to unravel the enmeshment of politics and belief to our common benefit? Or at least understand it better so it can be used for the common good?

PATHS TO BELIEF

Moving on from the reasons and causes for belief and why it is interlinked with the political, let us consider two processes (among many) that lead us to political belief in the first place. One may be seen as 'rational' by many and is loosely associated (or so we tend to believe) with the methods and processes of scientific method. The second relates to the interpretation of symbols, emotions, and other subconscious processes. These two blend to lesser or greater degrees in individuals and societies when it comes to political belief. Both go back to the root need for survival. A single individual or group may also use different blends of the two depending on other factors. So we are looking at two ingredients that mix in different ways, depending on contextual variables such as time, place, and culture and which vary from one individual to another.

'RATIONAL' BELIEF IN POLITICAL IDEAS

Without delving into the nature or debate around truth and belief in science, it's suffice to say here that scientific method allows scientists to reach conclusions about whether something is believable via a specific and agreed upon methodology. This also means that when future generations replace old theories with new ones, the former are not necessarily mistakes according to the standards of their own time and can be extremely valuable in themselves. The future disproving of a scientific theory does not mean that it has no value while it lasts. Quite the opposite. But because of the scientific process, these beautiful mistakes are also left behind in the sense that scientific progress allows for previously agreed upon facts to be replaced. An example is, 'the transition from Newtonian to Einsteinian mechanics [which] illustrates with particular clarity the scientific revolution as a displacement of the conceptual framework'.* We ascribe fact to something incorrect via a correct and agreed upon method of reasoning and reach consensus with others. A belief and ascription of truth that can one day be reversed with further experimentation, more convincing facts, new observations. The products of such 'mistakes' are invaluable and are a method of progress without which humanity would have been the poorer. It is worth noting that despite the arrival of new paradigms in physics, Newtonian concepts are still in use in many fields.

Similar but more problematic and much less rigorous processes apply outside the realm of scientific enquiry. In politics, one may reach the decision that a certain set of values or views are of use to solving sociopolitical problems. This can be the product of both analysis and experience. It can even have its own body of supporting research, academic literature, and ardent defenders: the political 'scientists'; the flailing alchemists of our times, most of whom peddle either narrow analysis or false gold. This is partly what leads to the 'politics as a solution mindset' that has marred the Bridge. It is a flawed path or tangent from scientific reasoning that leads to political belief; something we might take to be rational and 'scientific' but which is far from it. The proof is that, despite their failures, we passionately cling on to these beliefs in ways that scientists could never hold on to their theories. Furthermore, we continue to be deluded in part because historically they did give us products in the form of new ideas and concepts to use, just not always the products

* Kuhn, p. 102

of progress. Science and technology have given us most of the progress we enjoy.

In the philosophy of science, extreme free thinkers such as Feyerabend believed 'that privileging one conception of truth, rationality, or knowledge in the name of scientific objectivity runs the risk of imposing a repressive world view on members of other cultural groupings who do not share the same assumptions or intellectual framework'.* When we observe that thinkers in science (admittedly extreme ones) can doubt their truths in such a way, how is it that in politics we allow ourselves to be so lenient with our process and so harsh in our defence of what we believe in? Perhaps it is because we are entangled with emotion.

BELIEF AS AN EXTENSION OF EMOTION

Another non-exclusive pathway to belief is the interpretation of an emotion, symbol, or other subconscious mental process by extending it and giving it an image. We relate this image to something that may come from personal experience or the recounting of anecdotal occurrences that do not bear statistical consequences. For example, this can affect our views on policymaking for public safety. This in turn can influence our assessment of public safety laws or the representatives we choose.

When we experience an emotion such as fear, for example, we activate a need to survive. This, when associated with the political, may cause us to link things which are not linked. The immediate problem of street crime from a policymaking

* Maria Braghramian, "A Brief History of Relativism", in *Relativism: A Contemporary Anthology*, ed. Michael Krausz (Columbia, 2010) p. 42

perspective is one of data, statistics, budget and asset allocation, and administrative competence. Root causes of poverty and inequality also have their supporting empirical evidence, yet people on various sides of the political spectrum disagree on causes, tools, methods, and desired outcomes. This is because emotion contributes to a pre-existing belief, leading to a perceived truth which is tangential to the facts. The same goes for hope, another emotion, which in politics is associated with an increased probability of safety. Thus both the emotions of hope and fear are linked to the same primal need: to survive. This is all influenced by our grouping and environment and can be subconscious. We believe we are observing a link but we are actually doing the process of linking.

Emotions themselves are truths by virtue of experience and consensus. They also have measurable chemical effects on the brain. So they are not a belief in and of themselves. Emotions are real because they do not need words. Fear is real without description or being given the name 'fear'. Nevertheless, they are given words and definitions, discussed, explained and, more importantly, extended. We have used language to explain emotions and that has caused belief. There is an entanglement between emotion and the political that is entirely natural, regularly dangerous, unavoidable, and at times highly valuable (empathy). But whether or not belief is to remain a component of that relationship is something worth considering.

WHAT NEXT FOR POLITICAL BELIEF?

The two paths to political belief are combined in ways that mean that we come to believe in politics. Problems that can be solved using data, scientific method, technology, and rational policy are clouded by false hopes and fears. Yet we must recognise that politics (as we understand it today) devoid of any belief at all is unimaginable. Because asking ourselves to make a complete split between belief and the political would remove a component of what it means for us to be human. Recognition of our irrationality may have to suffice.

Yet, there can be a way for humankind to guide this entangled rope and channel it in a direction that allows for progress and finds a healthy occupation for our political belief. We admit the requirement for belief in politics, we embrace it on the condition that it is not dangerous. How are we to do that? How do we manage this need? First, we apply mechanisms of R in which we consciously ascribe belief to the value of these mechanisms and not ideas or solutions, because a mechanism is a tool devoid of values and thus is something pure in itself. Second, we create new methods of grouping and organisation that ensure survival. Third, we develop a new path to belief which alters its meaning. Fourth, we anticipate the coming change in our relationship to the political ideas of the Bridge (BPB) in a new RP.

THE THIRD PATH TO BELIEF: ASCRIPTION

Having recognised the pernicious irrationality of the extension of emotion and our inability and lack of desire to consistently apply rigorous scientific standards in our daily interactions with the political, we look to manage the need to believe by redirecting it. Redirection made possible by new equality of R and new methods of grouping and organisation.

We can consciously choose to believe in something for a specific reason. Here, the specific reason is that it increases our new group's chances of survival over other political beliefs. We recognise the value of belief to our psychological and social well-being and that of groups. We need to ascribe belief to something because absence of belief is denying ourselves a basic human comfort. We all need a blanket to shelter us from the cold but we must have the correct one for the climate around us. We also recognise that as humans we are naturally predisposed to believe. And so we 'ascribe' so that we are neither nihilist nor fool. How do we do this safely? In politics and Directorship, we choose to believe in a mechanism. That of DR.

Belief via ascription involves a conscious reasoned leap of faith after taking into consideration the possibilities of a new paradigm. However, being conscious of something does not automatically justify it. One must first subscribe to Directorship out of a 'rational' view that the world one imagines in a new paradigm is worth building. Then one accepts one's natural, human irrationality, embraces the extension of the emotion of hope and attaches it to Directorship. A rupture from the belief systems of the Bridge, Directorship requires that the reasons for its embrace are radically different from those of the previous relationship to BPBs.

Directorship is a construction that we seek to build. It is, for now, a design draft or even less than that. Something constructed well can deserve belief. Conscious construction does not undermine the notion of belief; it reinforces it because we attach our leap of faith (having conceded that all belief involves such a leap) to something that we are going to construct ourselves. Belief in the new paradigm's anvil, where the hammer of vote will break, shape, and fashion a new world.

The difference between an ascribed belief and a false idol: the former is the result of a conscious process of construction that involves a leap of faith as a component of the process, while the latter is something that feels like or appears to be a belief but is not the outcome of the process of ascription. An acceptable 'political belief' involves consciously ascribing belief in a tool via a leap of faith. Theoretically, anything can be believed. It is how we reach the point of belief and why we ascribe it to specific things that matter.

Does this change the nature of belief? It changes our relationship with a word.

COMPETING PUBLIC BELIEFS

Political ideas today are both public in nature and designed to be shared. These differ from privately held beliefs, which one does not necessarily reflect in the public sphere. Nobody says, 'I have a political view that I share with no one, it is private and unrelated to my fellow humans' as the idea would therefore not be political in nature. Not only do we dangerously believe in political ideas but we also vote to agree on what we believe in when we 'vote in' a representative of a party or an ideology. This means that embedded in current modes of political organisation and representation there is the implicit notion that there must be consensus on belief at some level. This defines many aspects of politics and what it means for something to be political.

Some people seem to equate the progression of the 'canon' of political thought across time as equating with progress in thought. This is for the most part incorrect. What has happened is that political thought worked incredibly well during the beginning of the Bridge, and now we have reached paradigmatic crisis. Crisis in the Kuhnian sense. From an idea's perspective, fascism, communism, and our dysfunctional societal relationships with technology are key. The West has regularly thought itself impervious to other cultures' canons or ideas, but it is precisely because they take Bridgeist political ideas so seriously that they are in danger. People must free themselves of their canons and historical baggage. There has been an overflow of ideas and saturation in the Bridge, while old and dangerous ideas linger and rear their heads. There are too many purported and competing belief-based meta-frames in modern political thought and society, and it is only by choosing, individually, to wipe the slate clean together and usher in a new paradigm that we might deal with this group of things that holds us back.

Scientists, with the benefit of hindsight and the emergence of the history of science as a discipline, know that that they are right while knowing they will one day be wrong. Seen through the lens of the Kuhnian paradigm, the scientific truths of today may not live up to the standards, minds, or experiments of tomorrow. One must take the long view of history. Shifting to a new political paradigm will allow us to look back on the truths that, much like the Axis of Ancients, were once all-consuming and convincing.

A PATH TO TEMPORAL RELATIVISM

Temporal Relativism (TR) is a specific approach to the political thought, ideologies, and political beliefs of the Bridge. When removed from the context of the first RP and current modes of Organisation (O) and placed in Directorship, TR is the lens we look through at our 'old' political ideas. These ideas are demoted from being 'belief systems' or deserving ascription and become practical components to be used in addressing the problems of the day. Their value becomes practical and not inherent. The relative value of a specific BPB depends on the point in time when you ask and the problems you are seeking to address. Their relative value waxes and wanes with time because of their changing usefulness. Little is fully discarded; nothing is ever fully embraced.

Taking the time to understand the history of our ideas could emancipate us and propel us forward, freeing us from the notion of the progress of ideas. We do not need lots of new political ideas and neither do we need to revive old ones. We need to alter our relationship with political thought itself and with it, political thinking must change forever. Ideas will be much less forceful individually, and healthier collectively, while existing in a context where they contribute to progress and problem solving. The idea that no idea is special is an idea in itself. There are, for the self-aware, more or less useful ingredients for the right ideas to serve today. Very little is fundamentally useless, yet in the Bridgeist sense of the term neither is anything all-consuming and 'believed' in. We have said we don't need new ideas, but they come along anyway and so we need a context and framework to receive them in a similar way to our urgent need to reshape our societies to absorb the technologies and products of the science of the future and ensure positive uses.

There never used to be many ideas and life was nasty, brutish, and short (in the Hobbesian sense of the term) and so we latched onto ideas with all our hopes and dreams and in the process developed a method of interaction with them. We got infected. The idea is not the problem, it is the addiction and abusive relationship facilitated by their design. But now, in a time where we are materially better off, we engage with them in the same way despite having an abundance of options for the first time on a mass human scale. We need to shift consciously from embracing ideas as truths to embracing a mechanism in the context of TR. We reflect the results of our introspection onto the world via our Directorship. Asking ourselves: what is good for now? How do we best handle this issue?

Freeing ourselves from the established notion of the progress of ideas, we need to decide on one meta-frame and persist with it for an extended period of time to progress. And if this frame is a BPB, as has been repeatedly tried, it will be a disaster. And so it must be a mechanism. Bridgeist Political Beliefs are there. Although they are a fact, their monistic side is mitigated when viewed through the lens of TR, itself a component of our Directorship because the mechanism protects from ideas that exclude others and from beliefs which claim to be eternal. Currently, it is not the ideas that we deal with which are the problem, but the framework in which they are both created and dealt with. Temporal Relativism allows us to embrace truths from relativism without falling into the trap of accepting everything and tolerating unacceptable beliefs in the name of liberalism, which results in being devoured by someone else's more forceful truth.

People might ask questions such as 'is this BPB right or wrong?', 'why can't we just accept all BPBs?', or 'why should we tolerate other BPBs?' These are all the wrong questions in the context of a new RP. In Directorship, we only ascribe belief to the value of the mechanism. For indeed, we need to believe and we will make it healthy by attaching it to a vessel. A mere conduit. Directorship is our framework and within it, we embrace a soup of 'isms'. Ideas, thought, and ingredients that are most suited to the needs of the day. No ism is overarching, nothing is forever shunned. It is a conscious and organic process that keeps us away from phases, dilutes societal moments of madness, and lays the groundwork for an organically developed global world.

As the number of fashionable BPBs (whether revived, repurposed, or entirely new) multiplies, it will increasingly be difficult for academics to define certain set timeframes as 'ages of XYZ-BPB'. This is in many ways an already long-gone view of the world; but taking this process forward to its (hopeful) conclusion is that it may be that the world and its future history will no longer be defined in terms of its phases, ages, and moments of madness. This is the optimistic but possible evolution for our species into one that takes itself forward on a trend of progress in political thought and structure for the very long term.

Many political ideas are 'Western' or are perceived as such and tend to be rejected by most of humanity. Most humans do not see themselves as being 'Western'. Indeed they are not. That is one of the reasons there has been no true ideological paradigm in the Bridge.

The canon has, historically, shaped us. We have also self-consciously used it to share and guide us as individuals and, in some cases, societies (at least for the educated). Now almost everyone is educated and this should mean that we naturally become more conscious of our ideas and more self-aware, but what it is doing is diversifying political belief in a way that is becoming unrecognisable. There is entropy. The world is no longer a cluster of isolated societies, each with its own ideas, nor are we yet one world where we share the history and future of our ideas. We are in an unstable extended transition phase. How we get through this and evolve may come down to the process that we individually, and together, learn to manage our political ideas by moving from the unconscious to the conscious on a mass scale, The world is ready to start doing that. Personal experience shapes our political views, and societies are moulded by their political past. Today, no human is free of that societal baggage. Neither rejection nor a full embrace will do when it comes to the history of our ideas and the constructions of the Bridge.

Technology can enable everyone's unique viewpoint to be represented via full participation. The arguments about maturity, apathy, and practicality will fall. They only stand when you strive to either maintain a dictatorship, move from a dictatorship to representative democracy, or sustain an ailing democratic system. It is voting regularly, practising, seeing effects, and being responsible for failures that takes us forward. Seeing the world of politics from this 'issues viewpoint' does not mean there should be no political thought or philosophy. It just means an acknowledgement that societies need to select the most useful ingredients for the moment. It is a conscious selection of what is currently beneficial. The blend of the day where no BPB reigns supreme and the addition and removal of elements is conscious.

The use of the mechanism reduces the value of parts of a BPB to its relative temporal usefulness, and this is where they belong. A spectrum of usefulness for today. The disagreement between individuals revolves around where these BPBs (which are no longer BPBs in the way we once understood them) land on today's spectrum of usefulness, applicability, and therefore desirability. It also means that Directors can dissect and make a collage with them and thus extract maximum benefit.

LOOKING BACK TO MOVE FORWARD

Let us imagine for a moment that we intend to treat ourselves better as a species than we have done previously and rethink modes of O and R to our common advantage. To shape ourselves consciously. Individually, together. Knowing that as humans we are uniquely capable of rethinking conceptual frameworks and applying new ones. How do we proceed to take the first step towards rethinking our belief systems and structures in a way that seeks evolution as a consequence and not as a goal? To build something that is a genuine reflection of our potential selves which is neither imposed nor imaginary?

In realism 'we try to bring an external view into the determination of our conduct'.* I am not necessarily calling for realism in the sense that there is a philosophical school, but rather appropriating a tool because, with TR, Directors can do that.

Maybe we need to look back at our history and see it for what it is: 'baggage' in the neutral sense of the term. Ideas with a capital 'I' are things that we bring with us to a new paradigm; those that we have lived with for as long as individuals and societies have had ideas. They are useful baggage if viewed through the right lens and can be given a new context for us to use them in propelling us forward. What does it mean for someone to know the history of 'their' ideas? What might happen if we all allowed ourselves this level of personal introspection to do it? Perhaps we might decide to progress past a Bridgeist state-based conception of societies built on exclusion and intergroup friction.

---

* Thomas Nagel, "Value: Realism and Objectivity" in *Relativism: A Contemporary Anthology*, ed. Michael Krausz (Columbia, 2010) p. 325

The norm of telling us how to think or 'guiding' us in our RP is paternalistic, suffocating, and past its sell-by date. So first we need to uncover the past and present on an individual level, and if millions of people do it, societies change. Asking ourselves, 'what can we grow out of and reflect from our new viewpoint in a world of politics without delegated representation?' Because identity does not have to come from the nation or BPB, it can come from the self. The self, when seen through the lens of the history of one's ideas, is much more than a little cog in a modern nation-state. There are even parts of the nation that came before the current one that can be more important. The strands of history and thought that make up a person have so much to give that the anchor of the Bridgeist nation is much weaker and heavier than that waiting to be used. History moves forward, that is inevitable. If we see our ideas as being the product of history and existing at a point in history, the only way is forward. That we are the sum of our historical political ideas and can 'grow forwards'. Progress, aided by a new dimension to our use of technology via a change in the mechanisms of vote.

The only thing in which to ascribe belief for now is that there is a need to shift from what is only conscious to some to conscious to all. Individually, together. That we may not only reach our own conclusions but that the process will shape us into what we really are. So that 'one becomes what one is'.* A species with a unique power to see ourselves in the third person. One that can study itself consciously and grow, with people living with a self-conscious, personal notion of idea management. Nietzsche's 'Overman'

---

* Friedrich Nietzsche, "Ecce Homo", in *Nietzsche: The Anti-Christ, Ecce Homo, Twilight of the Idols and Other Writings*, ed. Aaron Ridley (CUP, 2005)

(Übermensch)* is only conceptual, unique, and 'special' in the Bridge where the human average hasn't yet reached its potential. In Directorship, the healthy parts of that 'overman' can be the norm. We do not want to be guided. Those who try to guide, fail us. And yet we will not take things in hand and guide ourselves. This needs to change.

How do we become collectively self-aware enough to feel confident to get started? We don't need to wait; we will learn as we go. Because there is almost no way we can do worse than our representatives have. We have had genocide, world wars, persecution, and nuclear bombs. At worst, it will just be more of the same.

As Wittgenstein said of another subject, 'Don't think, but look!'†. We owe it to ourselves to look at our political ideas with a clear eye and see them for what they are: baggage to be shed. This isn't about education; we are educated enough. We have enough ideas and they are ours. We have claimed them and own them. Directors are the canon and we make ideas useful because that is all they are, tools to use, with relative amounts of usefulness depending on the day and the task at hand. This also means that none of them are 'real'. It may seem obvious that they are not real in the way that we may think of mathematics as 'truth', but our behaviour suggests otherwise.

Society is only a grouping of individuals. The individuals reflected in vote are parts that make a whole no greater than the parts themselves. 1+1=1+1, ≠ 2, and especially not 3.

---

* Friedrich Nietzsche, *Thus Spoke Zarathustra* (CUP, 2011)

† Wittgenstein, Ludwig. *Philosophical Investigations*, trans. P. M. S. Hacker, G. E. M. Anscombe, and Joachim Schulte (Wiley, 2009) p. 36

ETUDES 2–5

Old Words and New Meanings

With the arrival of the new paradigm, ideas and concepts that do not yet exist will emerge. These will fix old problems and create new ones. There are also existing or 'old' words that will gain new meanings. Words such as belief, identity, purpose, the 'other', property, the economy, nation, sovereignty, executive branch, leadership, equality, and rights are just a few of those that will evolve. Some of these words and our relationships with them must evolve before we can become true Directors. We will need a few changes in us first so that we can evolve as part of the end of this paradigm. Without these changes, Directorship is but a shell. Below is an imagining of how some of these words could change with us and change us in the process.

ETUDE 2

On Law

Alas, where'er my eye may light,
It falls on ankle chains and scourges,
Perverted law's pernicious blight
And tearful serfdom's fruitless surges.
Where has authority unjust
In hazes thick with superstition
Not settled – slavery's dread emission
And rank vainglory's fateful lust?

Alexander Pushkin, 1817*

LAW AND PHILOSOPHERS

Through Absolutism, paradigmatically speaking, philosophers from antiquity viewed the law through a broadly similar lens. Plato, Aristotle, Aquinas, Hobbes, and others lived in a world where progress in the modern sense of the term was a slow-moving, imperceptible, and generally

* *The Complete Works of Alexander Pushkin*, ed. Ian Sproat (Milner & Co, 2000) vol. 1 p. 269

inexistent force. In a context where so many things appeared to be fixed (the divine, law, morals, and peoples) an idealised conception of what law was and ought to be arose. A perfect state to which 'the community should aspire but could never attain'.* In Plato's *Republic,* we find the original or first idealised political system. A fixed state of affairs which is 'best' and a world that does not change because there is no notion of progress as we know it. This concept reappears under various guises from Aquinas to Hobbes and forms a significant part of the legal and political thought of the Absolutist phase of the paradigm. These thinkers found themselves attempting to answer fundamental questions such as 'how should we live?' and other questions of law at a time of an extremely low human average, low Representation (R), and negligible scientific progress (relative to today). Their approach gave societies the ability to 'feel' a sense of progress by changing their laws or conceptualising them as moving towards an idealised 'eternal' state. It was their way of moving forwards.

It is only with Montaigne (1533–1592) towards the end of Absolutism that we begin to find an idea of the possibility that differing systems, mindsets, or 'worlds' might have relative virtues and no 'best' outcome; or that conceptions of law and their relative merits are not necessarily immovable or eternal. Aristotle had a conception of diversity in political systems, with his famous division into different labels, but there was little or no appreciation of things from what would today be called a relativist point of view. As the Western world shifted into the Bridge, humankind's perception of

* Huntington Cairns, *Legal Philosophy from Plato to Hegel* (Greenwood, 1980) p. 55

the law as a monolith to maintain or truth to be discovered faded, giving way to modern conceptions of liberty, the individual, and rights. The law became something men built (today there are thankfully more women involved but still not enough). Constructions of justice and edifices of thought both liberating people and pushing up the human average as well as forcing representatives to concede to it. In a world with true progress, the enactment or abolition of laws has allowed us to ride on a wave of change, steering us towards a freer, fairer future. We have had thinkers like John Locke and Jean-Jacques Rousseau; documents like the American Constitution and the French Declaration of the Rights of Man; laws such as Alexander II's emancipation of the serfs in 1861 enacted; and the significant victories of the American Civil Rights movement.

Despite many dark moments and numerous representatives full of evil (there have been good ones too), the general trend throughout the Bridge has been 'up'. Up in the sense that humanity has elevated itself. Much of the behaviour of representatives, well into the 20th century as well as in contemporary dictatorships, has been to either combat the march of freedom and equality or to give way while trying to retain power structures and a status quo that maintained their privilege. Systems that kept the R out of the hands of 'their' people. The story of the Bridge is the tale of the weak many against the powerful few. It is about normal people claiming their R and trying to create just societies and a world in which they want to live. It is also worth noting that there are many representatives today who do take part in the political process in ways that promote democratic norms and engage with the public with integrity. These, sadly, only represent a small percentage of the world's population.

LAW TODAY: THEORY VS PRACTICE

The 20th century at the end of the Bridge has been marked by great legal thinkers such as Ronald Dworkin and John Rawls. Minds whose works symbolise (irrespective of any potential agreements or divergence with their views) humankind achieving an elevated state, at least in the level of its thought. In practice, the mechanisms of legislation of the late Bridge are, across the globe, increasingly the tools of companies and private interests who own our representatives. Those that are relatively independent are either dictators, work for them, or have their re-election at the forefront of their decision-making. In other contexts, representatives form ideological groups (political parties) that reduce R and threaten democracy. Law in the late Bridge is increasingly a tool of elite financial interests as well as population control. I am not speaking of rampant conspiracy theories of attempts at secretive world government. Just, rather, the crushing day-in-day-out grind of a system that reinforces differences and weakens average people's R. The gains that marked the Bridge are beginning to be reversed. Technology may make these rollbacks permanent. The Bridge is ending and progressive legal minds are being left by the wayside making way for authoritarianism, abuse of power, and eventually changes in law that will bring about some of the basest facets of our humanity.

Worst of all, in most places, neither law nor the existing processes of lawmaking are allowing us to address the existential threat of climate change in ways that will yield the results we demand and need. We are being denied our last opportunity to ensure the integrity of our planetary ecosystem and allow ourselves an existence that doesn't bring to mind the way our cavemen ancestors found themselves at the mercy of ice ages. The thought of living on an off-planet world that has to spin to make its own gravity and where putrid human breath and excrement are recycled for us to re-ingest is simply nauseating. We will leave behind a planet that is totally ruined for us as well as trillions of other lifeforms to which we have shown no respect whatsoever. All because the most advanced and resourceful species choked when it knew what had to be done because some had too much R for the right laws to be made.

Looking across the globe today we find, in most places, the law in a sorry state. There are countless places where Dworkin's Hercules* is merely a petty king, representative of a political faction or accepter of bribes. Places where having the right lawyer means someone can win a court case despite being guilty and caught red-handed. Entire states where the law is but a reflection of the whims of a dictator, king, ruling class, or so influenced by commercial interests that companies pay lawmakers to have them elected to change laws that don't suit them and make ones that do. Presidents levy taxes on millions of people while their circle is exempt and they fill state coffers only to empty them through means made legal by corrupt legislators. There are of course places where the law is nothing but a tool of brazen repression and control and those in charge don't even need to deny it.

There are nations where there is little rule of law if at all and selective when applied. Dozens of such countries exist today and the number of victims is countless; victims of the

* Dworkins, in *Law's Empire*, describes an imaginary 'Hercules' or a certain model of a type of judge that has significant and perfect powers and capabilities.

law where they live. We find places where new ideas aren't welcome and the law, built on old ideals, is applied with zeal to contain and crush generations that have changed so much that the entire system has become obsolete and cruel. Antiquated notions of morality and social rigidity are imposed on those who think and feel entirely differently. A world where dogma holds sway because people have been trained to accept and follow conventions to reinforce oppressive systems. Here we are not speaking of abuses of law but rather of law itself or, more precisely, what laws shaped by rulers with too much R can look like for those under rule in the 21st century. There are nations where societal or religious norms become institutionalised and supersede the law. In these places, authorities ignore laws and legal precedents to enforce a socially accepted or imposed view of norms. Mass sentencing, torture, and extra judicial killings are, in some places, techniques that are used as enduring substitutes to parts of their legal system.

Depending on where you are, the law can have different meanings. In most places deep questions about law are neither asked nor have they been pondered on for a long time; except possibly by thinkers behind bars. When asked, the questions are often imported from places where the law is made and applied differently or mean something else entirely in a completely different legal culture. But the most significant gap is between the theory and practice of law. That is partly because theory is the basis of the system in only a minority of states, mostly in Western Europe. For most, it is a story of abuse of constitutions and laws as well as justice and rights by political classes and both their enablers and supporters. Abuses of R. These are places where the law is, by design, a tool of control and not much more. Most of us have never experienced anything close to *Law's Empire* as envisaged by Dworkin, or fairness as envisaged by Rawls, property rights as safe as Locke would have had them, or even stability like in Hobbes' *Leviathan*. Most of these things, for most of us, have never shown up. They may have informed some of the world's systems, but the law as an idea as understood in Anglo-Saxon countries or Western Europe is anomalous.

THE FUTURE OF LAW IN THE HANDS OF REPRESENTATIVES

The future of the law in the hands of representatives looks grim. The United States has shown that maintaining a separation of powers and democratic institutions depends on their goodwill. Concepts such as lobbying and others are used to abuse R legally. The United Kingdom's political class has failed their electorate on numerous levels in light of the Brexit vote, while on the continent, dangerous and parochial ideas from a time with a lower human average have resurfaced in the form of modernised nationalism. Many non-European states maintain and propagate ideas and political structures that reduce R while promoting and legitimising governments around the globe that strengthen laws of control. Almost everywhere the law is being paired with technological advances and control of the Internet to reduce R, freedom, and liberty. The control state has risen and is here with governments increasingly aligned on their shared interest in population control.

Could it be that the human average has become so high that it is dangerous? The answer, if you are a representative in a dictatorship, is yes. Most lawmakers at the end of the

Bridge do not make laws for the benefit of the electorate, but to reverse the latest round of freedoms won by the generations that have enjoyed a free Internet but have yet to cure its ills. Instead, we are being robbed of liberty itself.

Let us for a moment leave the gritty realities of the late Bridge and return to the suspended reality of philosophers who ask questions such as 'what is law?' and 'what is justice?' Let us remember for the stretch of the next few pages that we are looking to make a new paradigm so that we can allow ourselves to rethink fundamentals and build a future worth living for all. What ideas then, could inform a theory of law for Directorship?

WHAT IS LAW?

Is law a thing in and of itself or something derived from its purpose? Or is law a consequence? If so, of what?

If law is a thing in and of itself, then it exists independently of humanity. We find it and don't make it (e.g. natural law or the laws of nature/physics).

Such law could not have an inherent purpose because it simply 'is'. We would be giving it purpose by virtue of our interaction with and discovery of it. Alternatively, it may be that the law 'is' but is altered either by our interaction with it or our observation. A bit like Schrödinger's cat who is only dead when we look. This notion of law without purpose is silly because without purpose it is not law (unless law is nothing but a logic game). So could it be that there is indeed a mathematical structure, a perfect system of law to discover? One where everything is balanced and set out? Even if there were, it would be perfect in that the relationships within the system were perfect, but its application and interaction with humans would mean it becomes imperfect because it is given purpose. It would be something perfect in and of itself but not perfect for humanity.

One can imagine a computer that has made perfectly fair rules or laws, like a game, and because of this perfection (of the type that pleases mathematicians and physicists), it is applied to humanity. It becomes the law. An AI that is law book, prosecutor, defence, judge, and jury that holds all the answers derived from a set of principles and perfect rules and the answer is always either found there or derived from it. We have a nascent version of parts of that in Dworkin's conception that the law already has all of the answers and that Hercules will find you the right one. The problem that we face is that this system of perfect rules is no longer perfect once it is given purpose other than existence within a suspended space, far from reality. Its interaction with humanity causes distortions and when imposed on the lives of billions of people, its state of perfection ends and hence the conceptual awe and respect we hold for it. These systems are devoid of humanity; cold and perfect and yet incompatible for the purposes for which humans need laws.

Laws for humans made by humans arise from need. This need can be real, imagined, or anticipated. It is a response to a need. The needs of humans. Laws made for us, unlike those of science, do not need an inherent quasi-mathematical logic nor can there be a perfect state of law that is discovered or even invented. Systems of law are therefore not something independent of us. They are shaped by us (or for now by our betters) and shape us in turn. Law is not about a science of relationships between laws. A system of law must, in essence, fulfil a purpose or a set of purposes. This purpose is to respond to a need or set of needs. A law achieves its purpose when it fulfils the need for which it was enacted in response. But what then is the purpose of law? And what purposes could or should it serve?

PURPOSES OF LAW

We are doing the opposite of looking for a perfect state of law. We are looking for a perfect means of progress. This section does not seek to cover the law in its entirety. That there is a focus on certain aspects of the law does not in any way mean that the parts left aside are either unimportant or too vast to be dealt with here. This is not an exhaustive account of what may change but rather an attempt to see how a sample of things could evolve in a new paradigm where Directors make the law for themselves.

DEFINITIONS

Definitions are important because defining is a core purpose of law. The law exists, in many ways, to define things. By defining them they either come into being or are extinguished. Some things either exist or don't because they are either defined or cast aside by law. In that sense, legislation can be seen as a tool of creation and destruction; of groups, individuals, and ideas. These are powers we seek to democratise to ensure the safeguarding of all individuals and groups. The act of definition creates by naming and then either legitimising or denying, and destroys by either ignoring or purposely denying something's existence.

FREEDOM AND CONTROL

A central purpose of law has been to balance freedom and control. The fact that control is at all a dimension of the law has much to do with the nature of our paradigm and the existence of representatives. Control is legitimised through law. This is not a fundamentally bad or evil thing but the reasons for control are becoming increasingly untenable. Control or the need to control emanates from fundamental problems of hierarchy and is, therefore, a problem of Organisation (O). Hierarchy today is abuse of R. It shapes people and humanity. The law creates groups, eliminates others by not acknowledging them, and controls the interactions between them.

Focusing here on internal group interactions and political laws: what has hitherto been the purpose of law in much of the Bridge and contemporary dictatorships? To cajole and coerce, to control and dominate. It has served a governing purpose and its application has led to too many negative outcomes throughout history. Could this change? In a world without representatives and changes to hierarchy, this purpose would reshape itself and conceptions of sovereignty entirely.

Law is also something that both defines and is affected by O. Freedom and control is a consequence of the problem of hierarchy which informs law and is supported by it. With the Enlightenment 'the liberation of the individual from feudal social hierarchies – as well as the liberation of the human mind from self-serving clerical dogmas – represented the birth of modernity'.* How then do we take this forward and develop structures which truly set us free? We must seek to elevate ourselves as a species.

* Larry Siedentop, *Inventing the Individual* (Penguin, 2014) p. 8

ELEVATION AND DEMOTION

A core purpose of law is to create and regulate human hierarchies as well as our relationships with and between entities. This has been done through laws of 'elevation and demotion'. Almost any law and entire legal systems can be seen as furthering the purpose of one of these two directions. These two processes control the notion of rank and status within societies. It may appear, at the outset at least, that such concepts are outdated in Western societies, and yet they continue to inform key areas of social interactions which have a source in law. In other places, such notions still hold strong in both law and society.

Rank and status are important to examine in the context of rights. People of equally high rank and status enjoy dignity and, by extension, equal rights. Directorship seeks a source of rights that holds stronger than the theoretical foundations ascribed to them in the Bridge because human rights have failed billions of people. Throughout history, there have been laws whose purpose has been to elevate with others being used to demote. The worst have put single individuals above all others while giving the rest an equally miserable low status. The best have been the laws that have equalised while elevating those on a 'lower' level, but very few systems have undertaken to elevate humanity itself. Not just the average, not just a few, or many, but all of us. To bring us forward to become something new and make human rights unquestionable.

The philosopher Larry Siedentop tells us that:

> *In Paul's writings we see the emergence of a new sense of justice, founded on the assumption of a moral equality rather than on natural inequality.*

> *Justice now speaks to an upright will, rather than describing a situation where everything is in its 'proper' or fated place [...] in his vision of Jesus, Paul discovered a moral reality which enabled him to lay the foundation for a new, universal social role.*[*]

Christianity broke with ancient wisdom that said that we are, as humans, fundamentally unequal. Despite this and the shift of most of Europe to Christendom by the end of Absolutism, humanity's equality was to a great extent left behind in law and practice. Vertical hierarchies abounded and it was only with the arrival of the Bridge that things started to become slightly more horizontal. Flatter structures. Despite increasing equality of rank, status, and dignity, human rights have not been able to stem some of our more atrocious behaviour in the Bridge. Many of the odious events witnessed as recently as the 20th and 21st centuries attest to that. It seems that the grounding of human rights in natural law, conceptions of moral equality, and other ideas have proven to be weak in practice and unable to shield people from harm.

How then, might we use our new-found vocation as law-makers to inform a new theory of rights? Lawmakers today enjoy rank, status and, for the most part, a certain amount of dignity. This stems from a very old notion that Directors will bring back. We will appropriate across time, bringing back old things and making them anew.[†] We look to Aristotle's conception of nobility through vocation. That what you do for a living shapes you. This lies at the core of rank, status, dignity, and therefore equality and rights.

---

* Ibid., p. 66

† See etude on culture in this book, pp. 167–173

RANK, STATUS, AND DIGNITY

Historically, rank within social hierarchies was ascribed, to a great extent, by birth or bloodline. Aristocrats would hold higher ranks by virtue of their lineage than peasants or commoners. Such hierarchies were enshrined in and regulated by law. Over time and especially in Western societies, notions of rank have changed. Jeremy Waldron, in his book *Dignity, Rank, and Rights*[*] tells us that dignity emanates from status and that historically, 'a nobleman might insist as a matter of dignity on a right to be consulted, a right to have his voice reckoned with and counted in great affairs of state'. If we generalise this (and really generalise it) giving everyone a right to have his or her voice reckoned with and counted in great affairs of state, then what was formerly a high and haughty prerogative might come to seem mundane as the ordinary democratic vote accorded to tens of millions of citizens. Today many citizens sometimes complain that their votes are meaningless and many philosophers support their complaints. But the dignity hypothesis reminds us that, although it is shared with millions of others, this vote is not a little thing. It too can be understood in a more momentous way, as the entitlement of each person, as part of his or her dignity as an (equal) peer of the realm, to be consulted in public affairs ... the transvaluation of older notions of rank.

This status-centric account of dignity speaks of it as being 'a principle of morality and a principle of law'.[†] Laws and lawmaking are seen as tools for the elevation of humanity to

---

* Jeremy Waldron et al., *Dignity, Rank, and Rights* (OUP, 2015)

† Ibid., p. 13

equally high rank. Here we focus on the content of the law itself as a mechanism for achieving such high status for all.

Waldron proceeds to tell us that:

> *[...] high status can be universalised and still remain high, as each of an array of millions of people regards him- or herself (and all of the others) as a locus of respect, as a self-originating source of legal and moral claims. We all stand proud, and – if I may be permitted a paradox – we all look up to each other from a position of upright equality.*[*]

This statement is firmly rooted in some of the most honourable thought the Bridge has given us. It is truly democratic in sentiment and seeks to elevate. A problem arises when it comes to rights. Human rights in the Bridge, for the most part, call upon a conceptual moral equality that stems from concepts derived from natural law. While one may welcome such ideas and even agree with their content, the weakness of human rights stems from their source. Rights try to give people 'a rank assigned now to every human person, equally without discrimination: dignity as nobility for the common man'.[†] The problem here is that rights do not actually give us this dignity consistently in practice. It is precisely because they are allocated or given by the wrong source that they are not embraced on all four corners of the map. How then can we acquire and develop this legal dignity instead of being 'given' it?

---

* Ibid., p. 60
† Ibid., p. 22

The first step is to ensure that, following the tradition of some Bridgeist nations, notions of equally high rank and status are enshrined in law. Directors must use their inalienable right of equal R to legislate for the elevation of humankind. This would change the source of our rights from a theoretical grounding to something approved by vote made real by the first legitimate legislators. One could argue that this is also 'giving' instead of 'acquiring', but the change in the source of law changes the concept entirely, making it something to be reckoned with in the physical world. In order to do this, we must look at hierarchy. If we are to put the individual at the top level while developing political structures that make this a net good, we must look to the remaining barriers that stand in our way. The most pressing of these are natural law, the nation, and the planet.

THE STATUS OF NATURAL LAW

Natural law is the idea that law and principles exist independently of human action. Highly conducive to progress in distant times, natural law ideas today do more to hinder than preserve. At its core, natural law is a problem of rank and therefore status. There is a body of law that exists, or that is by default 'above' humanity. We (and another problem is that we are seen as a 'we') are neither the source of law as individuals nor the sovereign in practice. Natural law places us lower than it by virtue of its source. This weakness in the concept of natural law means it is regularly ignored in practice. Many people conveniently don't respect it and defying it is defying something that isn't there to defend itself. This is similar to a god (or an idolised set of ideas) who, just like us mere mortals, has hitherto relied on representatives. Imagine instead an aspiring dictator expressly trying to go against the recorded will of billions of registered voters. Natural law and therefore issues of sovereignty, while having done so much in the Bridge to elevate us, now stand in the way of the evolution of our status, dignity, equality, and rights to a higher level.

THE NATION IN HIERARCHY

There exists today, in many places, the notion that nations as entities have status or dignity. That they are a thing in and of themselves and require status. They sit above us mere citizens and subjects. They are, for nationalists, to be treated almost as gods. The inherent dignity of the state is a longstanding and entrenched fabrication. There are many leaders in the developing world who think in terms of 'country rights' and seem outraged at the idea that mere individuals would 'erode' these to gain a misplaced, 'foreign' sense of human rights that they don't really need. In some places (many of them 'advanced'), entire systems of law are built for the preservation of the nation, state, and its structure. This might not surprise an end-of-Bridge reader. It is a 'natural' component of our political environment and part and parcel of the paradigm. And yet with the right progress, could such a concept one day appear to be old, antiquated, and mediaeval in its role in degrading the status of the individual?

WHERE ON EARTH IS THE PLANET?

We face humanity-defining problems with our climate, ecology, and the difficulties that we have caused for the Earth and ourselves. The notion of the planet as a single ecosystem or 'thing' in itself is relatively new and has come to inform our understanding of how actions in one place affect the whole world. As we progress at snail's pace (and sometimes regress rapidly) towards what is either reducing carbon emissions or our collective doom (none of the problems discussed in this book matter if we all suffocate), the Earth may require higher rank and status than us in law if we are to save it and ourselves. Here we are faced with a major dilemma. Not elevating the planet to what many agree is a well-deserved status in the face of crisis could cause Directors to legislate too conservatively to solve the problems at hand. On the other hand, ranking the planet above humans, while tempting, poses the problem of simply replacing the concept of 'nation-above humans' with something else. This would risk merely replacing one hierarchy with another. One can imagine a world where, with the wrong ideas and structures, crimes are committed in the name of an overcrowded planet. We must beware the new idol on the pedestal, and yet we should do everything we can to protect what is both our home and that of trillions of other lifeforms. That is a matter of duty. Could it be that if we rank ourselves sufficiently high, that the right of living in a clean and safe environment would lead us to legislate for the planet on purely selfish grounds? If we could find a way to balance priorities, things could go well. Legislating for the Earth as a consequence of the need to protect ourselves.

The Copernican model put the sun, as opposed to Earth, at the centre of the universe. This meant a fundamental reordering of our position in relation to other entities in space. Symbolically, it signifies the depth of the mindset change that Directorship seeks to achieve. The individual is to be placed at the centre of the universe; not a state, nor an idea, or collective, or group, but the individual. The notion of the primacy of the individual is key to the ideas that will take us forward. Our conception of equality and rights also emanates from putting each person in an equally central position. A shared centre. We seek to preserve and elevate each individual's humanity. Rights and equality through dignity that we create through vote, changing the nature and role of the state and law. Society becomes, genuinely, the sum of the individuals within, but nothing more.

ANIMAL STATUS

What could Directorship mean for animals' rights? For the most sceptical of us, how about the suggestion that while we elevate ourselves to something entirely new, we drag animal rights with us, giving them the same rights we gave our old selves? Could Bridgeist human rights for animals without equality be a compromise everyone could vote for?

STATUS THROUGH VOCATION

The second leg of our journey in search of a truly elevated status and dignity for humanity as a whole lies in the lens through which we frame our new-found vocation as law-makers. Elevation through legislation does not only mean the content or source of the law but that the practice of being lawmakers can itself elevate us towards having status and dignity that give us the correct meaning of equality and undeniable rights for all humans.

Western notions of status are infused with the concept of nobility of vocation. In modern times, one's 'function' in society can define people's perception of status (this is itself a reflection of an abysmal attitude). Many societies go so far as to use the names of certain jobs or vocations as insults. Conversely, there are jobs which appear to many to have an inherent dignity such as being a judge (law-related), and others involve status which gives dignity, such as being a public notary (also law-related). While the downside of this facet of our hierarchical mindset is, in fact, revolting, there are two aspects worth considering. First, as time passes, many of the 'lower' (to use an abhorrent yet commonly used term) jobs will become obsolete because such functions will have been automated. The second aspect is that, if we are indeed prejudiced to view professions in terms of their relative status or even as having inherent hierarchical connotations, we may yet turn this negativity around to have it play a positive societal role.

Legislation today, especially legislative assemblies and other representatives who play a role in shaping the law, has, in many places, lost its lustre. There is so much undignified behaviour, both in terms of the personal mannerisms of legislators and abuses of R by entire parties and legislatures that one may say that their status is increasingly eroded with every day that passes and that their dignity is not worth what it once was. How then, do we bring back the dignity in legislation?* The status is there, but it has been made impure by

* Waldron's book, *The Dignity of Legislation* (CUP, 1999) explores paths to restoring legislation's dignity within Bridgeist frameworks.

undignified and corrupt representatives. One needs only to call to mind end-of-Bridge American legislatures and executives with their horse-trading and partisanship to understand what it means to have representatives who serve ideologies as well as their personal financial interests.

Until quite recently, the legislator held an important and elevated rank in society. Something reflected in aspects of legal immunities from prosecution that recall, to a certain extent, some of the privileges of aristocrats of old. How then do we bring this dignity back? Ironically, the answer may lie with the Axis of Ancients whom we have been so desperate to move on from. We draw on the Aristotelian conception of nobility and dignity from vocation. That it is what you do that cultivates your mind and self. If we follow this, we ascribe a noble vocation for all of humanity. We can reach back to the Axis of Ancients and democratise things they held for but a few. In this, we take a few steps back to jump forwards.

We would gain dignity from our new, shared profession. We will be lawmakers. Being equal within it also makes it the ultimate equaliser. A truly equal R. We must cultivate our dignity by our vocation: lawmaking. Once the preserve of gods, god kings, lords, and others of high rank, we will achieve this rank individually together, elevating us all by our vocation and new-found identity anchor. From there we will naturally codify into law the rights that have hitherto been seen as the source of dignity. We will use our dignity to make rights that suit our new dignified selves. The concepts that we will normalise and enshrine in law were things once seen to be privileges. In turn, we must have the corresponding responsibilities. We must vote, we must learn, and we must legislate. If we do not perform our duties or behave as end-of-Bridge representatives have, then we cheapen the Director and the dignity derived from the vocation of legislator.

An important chapter in *The Dignity of Legislation*[*] tells us that despite himself and his prejudices, Aristotle couldn't help but tacitly admit or hint with hesitation and incredulity that larger groups of decision-makers might be better. That the whole of a people might be better. By whole, he limited that to male citizens (being from another time), but the point is that it almost appears as if Aristotle either did not want to believe it or that, because of the human average or lack of technology, he could not imagine such a world. We, almost 2,500 years later, can. If we take this idea from Aristotle, we leave the axis bereft of anything worth taking that we haven't already. A final gift.

EQUALITY AND RIGHTS

Directorship is not just about equality before the law, but equality in making the law and in shaping its direction. Equality of R and self-representation as an unalienable right. We affirm this on the first day by what was previously called a 'referendum'. That (now regular) exercise of rights will need a new name. Why is it affirmed? And why is it the only absolute right? It is affirmed because we have, as Directors, changed the source of law, which is now, for the first time, legitimate. It was not made by representatives or an elite. Law so far has been paternal prescription. Men legislating for women, the old for the young, the rich for the poor. The list goes on. Of course, it would be great if we marry our reborn law with

* Ibid., p. 92

an experiential (learning by doing) approach, but that is a choice only Directors can decide to make individually and jointly. A lens for looking at things while reflecting on our societies to look forward and out of them. Recognising that we share more with others than we have differences. How will our societies define rights? Restrictions only? Negative rights? Positive rights? These are things for Directors to ponder as they legislate, and not for any individual from the Bridge to prescribe.

I will not say anything of gender, racial, or other types of equality about which the people of the late Bridge are rightly concerned. They are, in context, worth fighting for but they are also in many ways products of the first Representational Paradigm (RP). I write from the standpoint that all humans are equal. Period. One hopes that these types of inequalities will die out as we progress into the new paradigm.

We seek rights because of new-found status and vocation, not rights as a theoretical foundation to underpin our legal systems. We ensure the right to vote as a practical right that is not grounded in mysticism, theory, or even morality. It is the foundation stone upon which we choose to build our society. The right to self-representation and equality of R is the fundamental right and source of equality in the new paradigm. The only guaranteed right from which others emanate. The foundation laid on which to build.

There have been many types of equality pursued, guaranteed, and denied by societies in the Bridge. Many with noble goals and others without. Most have been focused on equality of outcome, or specific inequalities that are addressed only superficially while having structural roots, making changes merely cosmetic. There has not been enough focus on equality of starting point, because that means remaking the world. Equality of R is the beginning of the end of privilege* and many other inequalities as they are understood today. Inequitable distribution of R has been the fountainhead of all other inequalities. What other equalities and rights will Directors demand? Which inequalities will they allow? How will these fluctuate over time? Or will we grow and learn to expand our freedoms in our push to preserve and protect the right to equal R and Directorship?

The life of a slave is the saddest, most pitiful existence a human can endure. The worst loss of equality and outright theft of one's humanity. Such an individual is so because they face the ultimate inequality of R. If all humans are represented equally, we are all equal as the source of our laws. There is something fundamental about this, when coupled with better forms of O, which makes us truly equal in the most basic sense, and consequently from that 'other' equalities and rights can be made. We, as Directors, must legislate to preserve others in structures where we do so as a consequence of seeking to preserve ourselves, not at the expense of others because the structure of the organisation and inequality of R make it so. This could, one hopes, lead to a change in the ills suffered by minority groups in the Bridge. In the first RP, groups have fundamentally mistreated minorities of almost all kinds. One dares to dream of a world where, due to equality of R, elevated status and dignity for all, and a giant political superstructure (Directors as one group), we will all quickly experience what it means to be a minority on some issue or other and learn to respect each other. In our current context and paradigm, this is naive but in the

* The word 'Privilege' is used as understood in the West in the early 21st century.

paradigm of Directorship, perhaps we might have opportunities to build on concepts that today appear to be but mere fancy.

SELF-APPLICATION

Moving on from the purposes of law, there is another dimension that requires consideration. That is our relationship as individuals to the law itself. In a world where we all stand tall as lawmakers, the need for coercion may decrease, and we would embrace the law as something 'of us' that stands for us, as opposed to an oppressive system to be tricked and evaded. We move on from coercion of the majority to self-application of the majority and coercion of the few who err.

Depending on where we live, today we have concerns of inequality before the law despite the principle of equality. Or genuine inequality before the law. In Directorship there is not just an end to inequality of the law, there is equal ownership of the law. This fundamentally changes humanity's relationship with law and thus its concept. It is no longer something that is made to frame how we live, but rather something we make for ourselves to guide us into becoming who we decide we want to be. It could also act as a sort of scout that we send ahead to explore and we follow where we like and send it in new directions if our trials don't turn out in ways that we want.

In a system where people make the law for themselves, there will be a much higher understanding of the content of the law as well as a dramatic increase in self-application. This means a reduction in crime and also fundamental changes in sentences and penalties as well as incarceration rates. It is not that the current penalties in developed nations are necessarily lax or repressive, but rather that the law in many places is built as a political tool of hierarchical control and societal preservation. The law will remain as coercive as Directors decide it needs to be, but the brutality may disappear because people will not apply such things to themselves.

JUSTICE AND PUNISHMENT

One of the most important purposes of the law is its role as the guarantee of justice for a society or group or between them. This angle has, in many ways, received the most attention from legal thinkers in the late Bridge and there is so much that is valuable to bring with us into Directorship. Much of our source material is both comprehensive and noble. Here I will only briefly mention one aspect of what is a major subsection of the law. The future of punishment. The law is the arbiter of relationships between persons, entities, and the laws themselves. This regulatory role comes with the power to prescribe punishments. Much of the purpose of the law has been, as we have discussed, about coercion, revenge, and control, and yet no society can exist without appropriate and proportionate forms of legitimate punishment created and dealt by the law. The notion that we will never have anyone transgress because of their new role would be naive and is not suggested. But it could be that the reasons for transgression may change and that rates of crime will reduce, while never actually dying out.

The context within which we evaluate the crimes people commit and the severity with which the law metes out punishment will be new. We may find that because crime rates are lower in a fairer world, we will become more compassionate and understanding. Alternatively, it may be that we decide that it is precisely because no one is ignorant of the law, nor in need, that punishment is to be made severe. Irrespective of our views today on the needs of tomorrow, the future of punishment deserves serious attention. Punishment currently serves, in many aspects and many places, a social role. We must at least remove violence from punishment so that, among other reasons, it ceases to inform societal norms that possibly emanate indirectly from legal concepts. We may also wish to stop all incarceration and develop new understandings of punishment. But above all, we must stop brutalising people as part of their experience of a justice system. Directors have status, all of them, and we must all be at home with the law. Wrongdoing does not allow a person to be stripped of their Directorship. We must find new ways for the law to coerce by starting to review how and why it should do so in the first place.

LAW AS VOCATION

A new purpose of law in Directorship is its role as a source of vocation and income for humanity. The democratisation of legislation will mean not just involvement and the act of voting, but a commitment of time, thought, and effort to both education and process. We must not just legislate but learn to do so and take the time to research, debate, and reflect. We will be lawmakers and get paid for the journey that gets us there.

Changes in law may also lead to laws that democratise the process and application of law. We may choose to ask ourselves questions such as 'what is a judge?' and 'what is a jury?' We may all yet grow to become a Dworkinian Hercules if the context evolves well enough to endow us with the right qualities and education. We may go so far in how we change as to democratise the enforcement of the law in a context where words such as 'mob justice' and 'vigilantism' are old words from a bygone era, where the public actively enforces the law within a prescribed set of rules and laws. The idea today may sound strange, but that is only because we are from the Bridge.

MORALITY AND LAW

Although morality is arguably so much more than a question of law, there are two aspects that are relevant here. Morality is a question of law for Directors because the law can be used to impose moral values. This has been a consistent commitment on behalf of representatives throughout the first RP. Moving on from the Bridge, we may choose that, the need for control left behind, the imposition of morals should not be a component of our legal system. And yet the law plays a fundamental role in upholding the values of equal rank, dignity, and rights with which we have chosen to endow ourselves. The inherent morality of our laws, even when we do not seek to prescribe and proscribe, will shape us and we must be conscious of this and deal with a light-handed touch.

Law cannot be, for Directors, a vehicle to impose ideals or morals as understood in the Bridge because the society that we are working towards is not a reflection of a set of cultural norms and values in the Bridgeist sense. This might imply a backseat for the interference of law in people's lives in the first place. Because we are all so different and about to become even more multifaceted, we may seek to think of the law as a moral force but not from or sourced in morality. It is from itself and has inherent morality by virtue of its nature and source. It is not that we have morality and insert it into the law to infuse it with 'good'. It is a morality shaped by our laws, not our laws shaped by a monistic or even kaleidoscopic view of it. We may bring a different view of political belief, but morality must come with us and grow, lest we leave it behind completely. The change is that we seek a different source for it.

A NEW MEANING FOR LAW?

The British jurist Dennis Lloyd, in his book *The Idea of Law*,[*] stated that people who think law is necessary do so because they see people as inherently evil and are therefore unable to live peaceably without coercion and vice versa. The opposite view is that good people are made bad by their social conditions and part of that is the law itself. From there derives the implication, held in varying degrees by many philosophers such as Plato, Godwin, Marx, and others, that there would be no need for law at all in the right political structure and people.[†] Directors, on the other hand, hold that people, while being fundamentally good, will never have a perfect world and do not seek such a utopia. We seek a world of continuous improvement where self-application of the law has reached a

---

* Dennis Lloyd, *The Idea of Law* (Abe Books, 1964)

† Ibid., p. 13

point where our relationship with law is more of a guideline that we have written for ourselves.

What could be a new purpose for law? For self-applying Directors to agree on guidelines and what happens when we deviate from them as part of a system arising from the codification of the rules people have chosen to live by and apply to themselves.

What is law? It is a self-portrait. And lawmaking is the act of self-portraiture. We gaze upon our reflection and in doing so we create an image of ourselves. We are formed by it and by the process of making it.

Can the law change what it is? Yes. We are looking for will as law. This is not new and has been seen as the basis of most legal systems. With Directorship, we are just cutting out the intermediaries; the representatives. Law is not really law until it is made by the people who are to follow it. Until then what we take to be law are mechanisms of constraint and coexistence. Law is to become something different entirely in Directorship, an expression of a new humanity. Law will be something people will want to live by because it is theirs by virtue of their creating it.

CAUTION

How are we, as future Directors, to view the existing laws in the Bridge? We recognise that until we reach a world of equal R, we exist, at least for now, at the end of the Bridge. It is important to note that today's laws can be legitimate according to their standards. This means that, in democratic countries at least, rather than submitting to an unjust system, following a Bridgeist law is a practice in self-application. We are not simply going to stop obeying the law in the Bridge because it is not legitimate by Directorship's elevated standards. A law made before Directorship may be useful, practical, or even just. However, its source makes it illegitimate in the context of a new paradigm, and this is why we will vote to reaffirm things pending their change. We are not rejecting the past, just moving on from it. Breaking the world to build Directorship would undermine the principles of Directorship itself. Such behaviour would ensure that we become Directors in name only.

DEFINITIONS TO DEFINE US

There is a definition or re-definition that will be required from the law that will change everything within a generation of this book being written. Something that must not, under any circumstances, be either left to representatives or left outside law's reach. I speak of defining both life and humanity. Today, what is not human may appear to be something obviously not worth our attention. But the lines will blur. New things will exist and we may ask ourselves what is or is not human. We are speaking of developments in AI, robotics, and genetic engineering, and of things one cannot yet imagine because they haven't been invented. Even then we are at risk of not understanding what it is the eye beholds. It may even be invisible. We must be ready to define both life and humanity. This process of exclusion or inclusion may be the biggest legal decision humanity has ever faced. What is law? That which defines life and humanity. There must be an answer to 'what is life?' and 'what is human?' in the context of law for a world where the boundaries may become unclear. We may, one day, even need to decide what does and does not constitute death. Can a person whose body has died but had their consciousness uploaded to a computer continue to enjoy their assets, or must their inheritors await in perpetuity as their parent 'lives on'? That is one of the simpler questions, others we may not be able to imagine yet.

Law serves the purpose of playing an important role in helping us make sense of the world in which we live. To give a structure to the unstructured and to understand the unintelligible chaos that is existence. Technological change risks muddling our sense of what is 'us' and what is 'the other'. Directors as opposed to the non-human. We must harness the law's role in shaping the idea of humanity in a way that protects us and our sense of self from the first real 'other'.

LAW IN A CHANGING WORLD

A major challenge faced by legal systems today is the inability to keep up with technological change. Products, systems, and services arise, are sold, and spread at a rate of change that is increasing exponentially. Legislating to have frameworks that anticipate or at least keep up with these changes is proving to be increasingly difficult. There are many states today that simply make blanket changes to repress the products of the Internet age to maintain control. In other, freer places, legislatures do their best to keep up. Could it be that things will change so fast that entire bodies or sections of the law become obsolete before a 'national legislature' (assuming it is doing its job) can react? Law can no longer be seen as a pursuit of balance between stability and change. The law must be fluid, but it must be that that fluidity produces positive results because things do flow, and so we must all be involved. That will require education and a living wage to be paid not only to legislate but to learn how to do so.

EKKLESIA

Directors will need a forum to discuss, debate, and decide. A parliament of all. A place to do our work and express our views. The Ancient Athenians called their assembly 'Ekklesia'. They would meet (unlike us it was men only) on a hill called the Pnyx, from where they conducted their affairs. Directors need a Pnyx where they can meet and this must be online. We must have our assembly. Our forum. An Ekklesia that includes everyone who is of age.

FUTURE LAW

Directors will make the law. We will need ideas to use and apply in our new context. We must not forget the Bridge entirely. Looking back at the Bridge, we will realise that many fundamentally good ideas existed and can be drawn on. The difference is that they came about in an unsustainable context and that our context will make them reach their potential.

Directors will need to make decisions on core issues in the law such as justice and rights. These are things where the Bridge has given us a plethora of truly valuable thought because, although the legal systems of the Bridge are mostly repressive, much of the thought about the law (legal theory, philosophy of law, and jurisprudence) has so much in it that will set us free. Things will need to be adapted of course, but our new world has an amazing amount of source material on which to draw.

The process Directors will undertake will have three dimensions: affirmation, transformation, and creation, and this will apply to all lawmaking in the paradigm. The new world will not appear out of a vacuum. Places and structures have a history, and existing laws and vote by all must be used to affirm or transform these. Old ideas that we want to keep need reaffirming to become legitimate. Whether it is done gradually and cautiously or aggressively and radically are decisions Directors will make, and will also depend on how much of the old world we have to re-think to move to Directorship. New laws will also, of course, need to be created.

It would be dangerous and Bridgeist of us to decide that Bridgeist laws are illegitimate before Directorship becomes a reality of R and O. A Bridgeist law is to be held as legitimate despite its illegitimate source on the following grounds:

1. It is holding things together while Directorship is on its way;
2. It does not impede the arrival of Directorship.

This does not mean we should not challenge the laws we have or improve things while we wait. It means that we are not to undermine the world's legal systems by virtue of their illegitimate source. This may seem to be a contradiction, but what future rulers (everyone) don't want to have to face is a major clean-up of instability and unrest. The laws can run as long as they last then we change them. It may also be that we choose to keep many of the laws that exist intact, while we may want to keep others intact for now because the changes will be minor. Some will be removed or changed entirely and must wait their turn.

We may choose to make natural law truly natural, in the sense that it comes from the first genuinely legitimate source. In that sense, we are the natural law, replacing the once-divine. If we do that we may look to affirm and enshrine many beautiful principles that, in the Bridge, seem to emanate from 'outside of us' as well as being 'inherent in us', such as notions of human dignity and rights. We don't really have dignity until we choose for ourselves (R). We also cannot really have dignity in a world with hierarchies in which so few have high rank and status. We all deserve the respect of those who are currently of higher rank, and it is through our new vocation that we will learn to re-see ourselves and in doing so recognise a previously hidden facet of humanity's nobility. This isn't about fantasy or imagining legal ideals to ignore in reality. It is about having the power to make what we want happen.

ETUDE 3

Identity, Meaning, and Purpose

IDENTITY IN THE BRIDGE

Identity is, for many of us, a central concern of our lives. Whether we are infallibly sure of our identity or in a continuous search for it, and irrespective of whether we are conscious of it or not, we interact with the notion constantly. 'Individual identity', 'collective identity', and 'identity politics' are concepts that coexist, clash, and smother one another in both the personal and public spheres. They are ideas that share meanings and impinge upon each other. Our interaction with the concept of identity shapes a significant facet of our existence and the political. Identity itself is also a product of the Bridge. This is not a grand or deep statement but rather an observation that occurred in the 20th century and so is part of the Bridge. Gerald Izenberg, an historian of identity, tells us that 'identity is a new idea'.* This does not in any way suggest that people did not have identities before Erik Erikson gave the word its modern meaning in the 1950s,† but

* Gerald Izenberg, *Identity* (University of Pennsylvania Press, 2016) p. 1

† Ibid., pp. 1–2

rather that, like Kuhn although in a deeper sense, he changed something by giving it a name.

People have always had identities but did not necessarily reference them as being such. They were not as self-conscious as we are today. It was also hard to see forces that once changed too slowly over the span of a single lifetime to be perceived. People have always identified vis-à-vis the 'other'; the conscious notion goes back at least as far as Herodotus.[*] However, our modern relationship with identity is a product of two things: a historical trend and an event. The historical trend is nihilism, which Nietzsche identified as Western 'man' being 'pushed by an abysmal and abyss-making logic'[†] and from there losing meaning and purpose. God had died in people's minds and so they faced a life of incoherent or unstructured existence that was not defined by a core notion or purpose that gave meaning. With no 'anchor' to tie the self to and nihilism as the anchorless ship of life, many people started to feel adrift without meaning and purpose.

These changes, shocking to societies where ideas had not changed at a rate perceptible to the individual in thousands of years, suddenly had to contend with an increased rate of development starting with the Enlightenment. With the arrival of the printing press, ideas and identities started to 'move' along with a raised human average. Ideas disseminated and evolved at a pace which a single, 'normal' individual could 'see' and 'feel' within their lifetime and not just endure without awareness. People increasingly became conscious of their place in a context of ideas that were dynamic.

---

* Francois Hartog, *Le Miroir D'Hérodote: Essai Sur la Représentation de L'Autre* (Gallimard, 2001)

† Tracy B. Strong, (ed.) *Friedrich Nietzsche and the Politics of Transfiguration* (University of California Press, 1988) p. 10

Second, this process was exacerbated by the two world wars. The horrors and intensity of these conflicts displaced many of the remaining anchors that people had been holding on to. People saw the 'hell' they had stopped believing in and did not turn to God to ask 'why', because he was, as Nietzsche famously put it, 'dead'.[*] Many people who experienced the war, especially on the frontline, were set 'adrift in unmasterable anxiety'.[†] Something that appears to have seeped into general populations by the early 21st century.

Even so, the experience of the West does not speak for all of humanity. There are also ex-colonies, with total populations now numbering in the several billion, that were once dominated by the West. There, irreversible transfigurations were forced onto pre-existing, pre-Bridgeist identities. Something akin to the displacement and uprooting felt by veterans of the world wars. The Bridge is, after all, a product of the 'West'. In these ex-colonies, many ideas were suppressed or transformed and anchors ripped away, leaving a hollow feeling that has been replaced with bits of other things, imagined pasts, or they have been engulfed entirely by Western ideologies, religion, or hate.

There are also places where either God never died or was never there in the first place. In many of these places, ideas have been used to change people to reinforce structures from the Absolutist phase of the paradigm instead of 'progressing' into the Bridge. Places free of the deep scars of colonialism but devoid of a past that embraced Western ideas for long enough to change them permanently.

---

* Friedrich Nietzsche, *The Gay Science* (CUP, 2002) p. 109

† Izenberg, p. 106

Back in the West people struggled with ills that loss of purpose and meaning had thrust upon them. Thinkers interacted with the notion of identity. 'For the existentialists, identity was a temptation to overcome, for Erikson it was something positive to be achieved.'* People wrestled with their loss of meaning and purpose in ways that can only be described as brave yet futile. Trapped in the Bridge, we all fight wrapped in a straitjacket. Notions of group identity and its relationship to personal identity arose. Discussions about whether identities are external things that we internalise and 'become' or whether they are inherent; the idea that there is no humanity devoid of groups. Questions of whether there is a self at all or whether that is all there is. We have, at the end of the Bridge, asked ourselves many old questions through the lens of the late 20th century meanings of identity.

Identities have been things that we 'have'. They are the expression of sociohistorical forces that have acted to shape the self, and in so doing have smothered it for many of us. Identities have also become ideas in and of themselves and are latched onto and used as anchors, yet they change and move at an increasing rate. Identities are things (living ideas) in themselves. Ideas just like liberalism, fascism, and nationalism are external to us, and it is we who internalise them. Perhaps the Directors of a new Kuhnian paradigm might learn to treat identities as ideas and forces external to the self that one must interact with in a much healthier way than we do today.

---

* Ibid., p. 105

SELF AND COLLECTIVE

In the early 21st century, sociohistorical and technological forces have given seemingly fixed things visible fluidity (at least in most places). Self and group identities evolve and shift at such an alarming rate that with it, we ourselves have shifted at a pace that will soon become untenable, although we cannot see it because each individual anchors themselves as best they can. An old reflex for a new situation. We walk on the cliff's edge thinking we are on a wide path with signposts. We do this because we do not recognise the point at which we stand in the evolution of something that has existed since time immemorial. The increased rate of evolution of identities is itself a developing crisis in the Internet age. There is, if we stay in the first Representational Paradigm (RP), a coming fragmentation of identities. Identities that once appeared to form cohesive wholes will fragment into subgroups in an ever-increasing splintering. We will each be more unique than before yet neither free nor self-assured. The harder we hold on, the faster they will fragment and cease to be useful anchors. It will feel like we are holding onto shards of glass that splinter as we squeeze. Loss of purpose and therefore meaning are part of the crisis of our RP and if we allow ourselves to find purpose in the identity politics of today, there will be no winners. Seemingly fixed identities are gradually changing and accelerating in their rate of change, weakening in rigidity since the end of Absolutism, ripped apart by colonialism and world wars, and exacerbated by the Internet and its products.

We have tried to fill the holes left by decades of losses by imagining identity as a thing in and of itself. There is a reason why we managed to give something a word. We saw it when it changed. Like a bird in a thick-leafed tree, it had to move to be noticed. We only realised what it was when we lost its permanence because before that there were purpose-driven meaningful existences that gave identity. Identity was once a consequence, not a source of meaning. We now use identity in our search for meaning and purpose, enhanced by the Internet and interconnection to find things to anchor us. The very technology accelerating the fragmentation of identities. We are running on a treadmill that may start to move too fast for us to stay on.

Furthermore, the increasing clash of identities is a symptom of our unhealthy relationship with a concept that came about to replace important things that were lost. Historically speaking, our purpose used to be clear and gave meaning, which together shape identity. In antiquity, the existence of Greece and Rome's peoples revolved around a religious conception of family and the duties that this existence gave them.* Later on in the Middle Ages, a human's central purpose was to serve God; this gave meaning to everything. In both examples the world made sense to those living in it. From that their core identity was unconsciously shaped and automatically derived. The last part was not conscious, generally fixed, or slow-moving and so it had no word. This does not mean that people didn't identify or group with political things or have identity in the modern sense without the term or an understanding of the condition. Rather that they anchored to things that moved so slowly that they didn't feel the change. The anchors worked and the delusion of fixed identity or interacting with it as if it was not dangerous became ingrained. If there were sudden ruptures, they did not

---

* Siedentop, p. 13

have the words to understand because they had no conception of something wordless. Luther was not, to the Catholics of his time, a reformer, but rather a problem. Someone trying to push something that had, so far, appeared to be unmoving.

Societies are increasingly capable of shifting cultural or societal norms at high speed because of the interconnectedness of people through technology. Furthermore, we have a higher human average than before, and so larger numbers of people can process information and find identity anchors. An example of the increasing rate of change is the dramatic (positive) shift in views on LGBT+ people in the Western world that has occurred as the outcome of a long struggle for acceptance and equality. The 'final push' of the early 21st century has been by a society with conscious individuals pushing a large number of semi-conscious people. Those who have stood against it are perhaps the most aware of how the change has been conscious. This does not in any way make it less genuine, it simply demonstrates our capability to consciously evolve our mindsets.

Today, for the self-conscious, modern human, group identity suffocates our notion of the self and gives it a hollow meaning and little purpose. Therefore, no modern identity has ever overcome the others because they are built vis-à-vis the 'other'. They clash because they are built in opposition to each other and cannot exist without one another. Identity politics as understood in the early 21st century is the twisted expression of a species that has lost something and is now looking backwards to find it. Taking identity to be a 'thing', using it to search for meaning and from there deriving purpose. If only it were as simple as Theseus' exit from the labyrinth. We have no thread to follow backwards. We must learn to look ahead.

In the last hundred years, the worst cases of identity politics have led to mass murder, ethnic cleansing, and genocide. Intergroup interaction is defined to a large extent by identity. This has happened in part because there is more 'self' than there was when people had a purpose. We no longer accept that our purpose or meaning can be driven purely by a single, imposed purpose. We have become too complicated for that and yet have tried with a seemingly wide spectrum of Bridgeist ideas: fascism and communism, relativism and liberalism, etc. Ideas that either subsume or accept all others. Both types perish for different reasons. We anchor ourselves to whatever we can, and the closest tethers are our immediate groupings (fatally taken to be the true sources of identity and therefore meaning and purpose) or those that sociohistorical processes have made into reality such as race, religion, class, and 'ism'. This has fragmented our identity. People belong to several groups without having methods of internalisation or discernment that work for the modern human. We are 'owned' by several identities. We tend to either internalise everything or just one thing and there is not much space for the self. Even liberalism which is, to some, all about the self, is weak in the face of Absolutist ideas: it cannot last in its current form.

IDENTITY IN CRISIS

Identity is not just a crisis; it is in crisis. We also cannot wish all of this away like it never happened by willing a dynamic anchor to be fixed. The word 'identity' has been given meaning and it arose from the disappearance of a core component of our existence.

It is in crisis because we still behave like it is fixed while actually it is increasingly dynamic. It is so dynamic that our old way of interacting with it is redundant and increasingly dangerous. We are dealing with something that has changed with old reflexes and so our relationship to it must change. It is part of the greater crisis of the Bridge. It is one of the signs that the paradigm has ceased to work for us. And yet without a new RP, identity politics may be doomed to culminate in our self-destruction. An Armageddon that even the religious would not look to God for because we will be 100% responsible. And yet, as with everything human-made, it is not inevitable.

IDENTITY IN DIRECTORSHIP

The meaning of identity could change with the coming of a new paradigm. Far enough in, when the first Directors are long dead and those who live are born into a world without inequality of Representation (R), there will be what Kuhn called 'untranslatability'. Kafka will confuse even more than he confounds today and Nietzsche's Zarathustra may make more sense than the children of the original who still haunt us.

In RP1 we are, to a great extent, used by identities. We are, in many cases, conduits for the expression of forces. Many people see themselves as 'part of', or they associate with, a group identity. It is, in some cases, 'their identity'. In these instances, the line between the self and identity is blurred. Where is the self and where is the identity? What is external and what is internalised? This is only true because we allow it to be so. There is a significant difference between using an identity and being used by one. Identities can be tools if we can give them a job that is suitable.

We must also acknowledge that many of us are using a word in the wrong way. One may feel that the identity or set of identities in question make up one's self and give it self-expression. This suppression of the self in exchange for the sense of purpose given by Bridgeist identities is hollow. It may feel 'safe', but identities are becoming increasingly fluid. Perhaps there is a new way ahead for Directors in the second RP.

If we are to regain meaning, purpose, and mastery over identity, we must see that whether we behave as if there is a self separate from identity is a matter of choice. Choice happens to those who have a self. Those who have a self, do so by virtue of choosing to not be overwhelmed by something in flux that we can no longer grasp with our two hands because it changes shape so quickly that we succumb to it and let it take us where it wills.

Many people today don't behave as if they are separate from identity as an idea external to us, but rather that they are a product of it. We interact with identities as if they are ideas that exist independently of us in the first place. This demonstrates that they are separate from us and are not us. If we were merely conduits, then we would be as malleable as the forces are and there would be no friction. This friction demonstrates that they are external and merely ideas for us to shape and use.

Identity is a dynamic thing but many people perceive it as static or a 'thing' because of time, history, and because much comes from subconscious identification. Also, the notion of dynamic identity, something that changes, is naturally associated with being something to fear because identity has been used as an anchor. We may, therefore, 'want' or 'wish' it to be stable. It may also relate back to the causes of belief and the need to survive. People who attach themselves to Absolutist ideas and identities are currently perhaps those with most subconscious fear of the coming changes. They have experienced environments that give them greater hope of survival than others because of perceived stability, and so enjoy a delusion more comforting than those who face the prospects of freer places. Alternatively, they have suffered more in dictatorships than those who live in other places, and are adrift in the anxiety of people knowing, deep down, that their context cannot hold. They know that they may not survive in the modern Leviathan that keeps them so far yet, ironically, so close to a Hobbesian state of nature.

In the statement 'I identify with and believe in XYZ' the word 'identify' is acknowledged as the key reflex that needs to be isolated and moved on from. It is this notion that is so pernicious to us. The political identity anchors of the first decades of the 21st century (the isms) will feel remote once the world has moved on to greater things and people anchor themselves differently to identities derived from vocation and purpose.

Identity and 'identity crisis' and other end-of-Bridge concepts, when seen through the lens of RP and the Bridge can be seen as us having reached a point where 'who we are' is no longer imposed and yet we have not found tools and methods to coexist happily with the identities, self, and meanings that exist around us and within us. We are at an in-between phase, a Kafkaesque malaise between the ignorant self-assurance of the mediaeval friar and the comfort of chosen anchors giving freedom to explore and evolve in a healthy and dynamic way. Directorship may give us just that as part of the new paradigm. In RP2 we move on from the notion of identity as started by Erikson and move on from the Bridge entirely. We will be as self-assured and content as we were in the Absolutist paradigm but also aware of our new place in a new context. Done correctly, it should be beautiful. It will be based on equality of R with legislators who have purpose, anchoring to an identity that although a means is neither an end nor a seemingly static, slow-moving Bridge construct and, accordingly, we will evolve.

That we choose to see identities as things in and of themselves and not a thing that constitutes our 'self' may be the biggest shift in the meaning of identity that we have experienced since Erikson. They are things to contend with, absorb, reject, and change. We must learn to become selective and discern from a position of strength.

But what exactly could happen if Directorship becomes a shared component of everyone's identity? In Directorship, we all acquire the power of the legislator and become, essentially, colleagues. We gain what is now the power of the few. The power of creation. We will create laws, change them, mould them like clay, and control our common destiny. This shift means that we will come to see ourselves differently. We will have purpose, paid purpose, meaningful purpose. A purpose derived from a meaningful activity once reserved for gods, kings, and representatives. From it will arise a common, shared identity shaped by this purpose. The correct fountainhead of meaning. We will follow the correct sequence of purpose, meaning, and identity to get what we need. We will see ourselves as equally important, not equally unimportant or of varying levels of worth. In a world where humans, all of us, are the source of legislation, the old conception of natural law lapses. Positive law in the Bridgeist sense of 'these laws are real because our representatives and elites made them so' will cease to exist when we become the natural and only source of positive law. We will be active and the activity will shape us and, through this, something of Aristotle will be carried into the next paradigm. The laws we make will be real because enough people willed them to be and voted. We will have identity from meaningful purpose; from a common vocation or mechanism; from freedom and creation; and from an anchor that is a vehicle of expression. Identity from something that does not change because it is itself a source of change. We will drink the water at source instead of walking miles to a poisoned well. A stable anchor for our identities. The word 'identity' will change its meaning in the new paradigm. It should not be forced and cannot be stopped. Once we step into a world of equal R, everything will change.

With Directorship, we seek to end the chaos of identity politics without reverting to Absolutism and terror because currently those are only temporary solutions and they are revolting. Managed properly we gain a new vocation. Dampened by time, many old identities will die like estranged great aunts who we barely remember. We will not really mind. The political will be dominated by a shared anchor; an anchor unique in its permanence by virtue of it being a mechanism of empowerment. If we all share the same political identity, and it has the same bearing on other anchors, then we become closer to being one while contending with the identities that exist and arise.

People may debate whether I am right. What is important to remember, and that we tend to forget, is that that we are all, from Socrates to thinkers of the late Bridge, alchemists in a first, rudimentary, paradigm. None but the few who thought for us early in the paradigm and at the beginning of the Bridge saw much further than their toes.

FROM 'BRIDGE SELF' AND 'PROTEAN SELF' TO DIRECTOR

BRIDGE SELF

We are people of the Bridge and we stand on it as it contextualises our existence. We are 'Bridge people' in how we perceive and deal with purpose, meaning, and identity. It has caused us a lot of pain, both for the individual and society, but it has also been our awakening. There is a significant problem with nihilist thinkers in that they do not necessarily presume that the possibility of a future identity anchor will be of long-term value or even that having one is a possibility beyond nihilism itself. That is because they have been looking for the wrong thing. How do we develop a relationship with something that changes both it and us and lasts a paradigm? How do we find palatable anchors in the political without bringing back old ones, quashing people, or imposing a Bridgeist solution? It is through the mechanisms of Directorship that we will find the avenue to redefine these relationships.

PROTEAN SELF

The concept of the Protean self was conceived by the psychiatrist and author Robert Jay Lifton.* It is a Bridgeist theory

* Robert Jay Lifton, *The Protean Self: Human Resilience in an Age of Fragmentation* (Basic Books, 1993)

that is, much like Switzerland is in the realm of R and O, anomalous in our paradigm. It allows us to see a future without providing one.

Lifton is an American thinker who was born in the inter-war period. He has been described by Philip Pomper* as having arisen from a context of: 'Rapid shifts in cultural ambience. The experience of the Great Depression, World War II, The Holocaust of European Jewry, the invention and use of nuclear weapons, and more than two decades of warfare conducted by the US in Asia.'† In that sense Lifton is a product of the calamitous events that have informed many identities in the early 21st century.

Much of his work has focused on the ruptures in identities caused by cataclysmic societal events and their effect on the psyche. His theory of totalism relates to dictatorships and their responses to these ruptures. In short, he deals with the worst of what the Bridge has made us endure. Something he witnessed first-hand in his intensive fieldwork. And yet, whether these experiences appear to you to be relevant or distant, it is his product that we look at here. The 'Protean person', not their context. We seek tools to build what is new.

> *The term 'Protean' comes from 'Proteus', the figure in Greek mythology who could change his shape at will. The term self-process is especially apt when applied to the Protean person. He experiments with some fragments left over from traditional identities and with others conveyed to him from other cultures*

---

* Philip Pomper, *The Structure of Mind in History* (Columbia University Press, 1985)

† Ibid., p. 144

> *and newly emerging styles of life, on a torrent of imagery issuing from modern mass communication.*[*]

But why do they do this? Why does Lifton's Protean person become Protean in the first place? They do so because they must as a response to monism. They resist, and in resisting lose themselves, pulled out to sea with the tide they must swim. In doing so they claw at what they can, desperate for anchors, but all the anchors do is sink them, so the Protean person sheds them and swaps them out. Putting together pieces of what they can find. They are creative survivors.

Lifton's Protean man, as viewed by a Director, is as sorry an existence as those who delude themselves with the idea of fixed identity. In a world where people either live under dictatorships that impose monistic views or in freer places where the fragmentation of identities and our relationship with technology is changing us, we all become, to a greater or lesser extent, Lifton's Protean man. It seems that at the end of the Bridge, even the strong suffer what they must as identities overpower them. With the accelerating fragmentation of identities, we may all end up becoming who Lifton has condemned us to be by defining something for us. This is the danger of staying in the Bridge.

In his conception of humanity, Lifton offers 'the idea of renewal through the innate power of human imagination [...] "open change" as an ideal model, antithetical to totalistic impositions of change and the coercive reshaping of human identities [...] one might see this as his creative response to the phenomenon of totals'.[†] And yet the Protean person is unhappy.

---

* Ibid., p. 162

† Philip Pomper, p. 156

He is 'out of joint because the symbolic world is disjointed'* and so becomes a 'creative survivor'† and suffers because the anchor delusion is lost. Nothing is permanent, and he neither has the tools to select, nor an anchor to hold on to. He has the new reflexes of a second paradigm but lives in an old context. The problems of Proteans arise from their existence in the Bridge, not from their form. We live in the wrong world.

We are all either creative survivors or denialists (pretending that identities are fixed anchors). Many of us are a combination of the two, but how do we move past these sorry states and become something new? A new type of person, the Director, arises from equality of R and a new paradigm. Directors will be humanity made anew, and we will recreate ourselves and our world from the toolbox of the dying Bridge.

THE DIRECTOR: CREATOR AND DISCERNING COLLECTOR

The 'old person' of the Bridge cannot be maintained and the Protean man cannot be without suffering. Neither alone hold the key to the reformulation of our relationship with purpose, meaning, and identity. Directorship offers a resolution of sorts. A way forward from enslaved unconscious sufferer or Protean mess to an anchored creator.

Directorship is, in relation to identity, first and foremost a source of purpose. There is something to do that needs doing and it must be done. We must legislate and we must vote. This purpose, deep enough into the paradigm, will give meaning

* Ibid., p. 163

† Ibid., p. 164

and inform everything. From there we will have an identity anchor. The difference between it and political ideas of the old paradigm is that the mechanisms of direct democracy and the meaning of the political will be neutral in the sense that they are neither a solution nor a made-up miracle. They are tools we use which in turn help to define those who use them. Direct democracy is the tool and Directorship is the context. The carpenter's tools have little or no use outside of his workshop. And if they are taken elsewhere, they tend to either not serve well or get damaged.

How is it that we can claim that Directorship is static if it is itself an agent of change? It is static specifically because it is not an identity, it is a purpose. We will experience this purpose for as long as we use the tools. We will have an anchor that works for our RP1 reflexes and because it is not dangerous in and of itself. It is merely a vessel for the expression of our new selves.

Unlike the monistic ideas of the current paradigm, Directorship neither tells us what to do, how to think, nor how to live. It offers no guidance but simply provides us with the tools to at first endure life and eventually enjoy freedom. It is, for those whose minds are stuck in the Bridge, something to fear. It is brutal because it forces us to grow out of ourselves and yet, coupled with the right organisational structure for politics, could become the first true vision of accepting most of the spectrum of viewpoints and their relative merits under a benign yet all-encompassing meta-frame. A child who, in the spirit of Isaiah Berlin's essay on knowing one great thing as well as many small things, grows up to be both Fox and Hedgehog.*

---

* Isaiah Berlin, *The Hedgehog and the Fox* (Phoenix, 1999)

Directorship could give us an identity derived from meaningful activity taken from shared purpose. We would become creators. In Nietzschean terms what is Dionysian in us will thrive and be balanced by the Apollonian of a new political meta-frame. In turn, the creator becomes an identity which we will all share. We will, for the first time, acknowledge that we share more than mere biology with those who we once felt were 'other'. We will be defined by our shared vocation and equally fulfilled role in it. A shared identity for humanity beyond what has clearly not been sufficient to stop us from waging war with each other. We can become our new selves while being better anchored to each other. A truly free but anchored individual connected to all humans. In the new world of Directorship we are ourselves and not agents of identities, and we choose our anchors because the structure of things finally allows this. We could be beautiful as a species, not just as individuals.

The creator is an identity. The Proteanism of the now anchored individual is the basis of our second identity anchor. Safe to explore, the Protean in us can learn to interact with the external, the identities that confront us, just as a discerning collector approaches works of art. Safe and grounded, they discover and discern. Shaping the rest of themselves, selecting from what they find, what they inherited but chose to keep, and what they wish to imagine and create. They shed as they evolve and use other identities to benefit their 'self'. We cannot pretend that Directorship will be the only identity we interact with and internalise (once it becomes an identity). There is, after all, a world out there. A world of ideas, languages, cultures, mindsets, forces, and things to contend with. The Protean in us caused by the Bridge can thrive in good health and shed its Liftonian meaning. A sort of 'Proteus appropriated' with a new meaning for an existing word meaning an anchored person with healthy Protean attributes. The new Proteanism is itself a source of purpose, gives meaning to things, and an identity. It is an attribute that contributes to our definition of what it is to be human. It also gives us a second thing to do. We now have two stable anchors for Directors. The creator and the collector. A new human, unrecognisable from the distant Bridge. A destiny.

For the collector in us, identities are things that the self accumulates and sheds and swaps and uses and treats as tools of self-reflection, development, and progress. With ascription and Temporal Relativism (TR), and Directorship as an anchor, it can be beautiful. Will you lose people or things in the interim? Yes, but you will gain an identity as a Director and be part of a new group. Directorship has within it the two unifying identity anchors of humanity that allow us to free ourselves of 'others', especially its political conception in the Bridge. Collecting (Proteanism redefined) is not compulsory. One may choose to become consumed with legislation. To become a permanent means. It may even prove to be a nobler path. A purer destiny.

The structure of Directorship is the true path to tolerance and compassion because in Directorship someone 'different' stops being the 'other'. They are the same in their cores as a creator but unique and on their own path. They are seen as being at a point on their path but not 'different'.

Evolution will keep us away from the anxieties caused by the feelings of societal stagnation. It is from stagnation that we seek to preserve and entrench things. Anything that is alive and evolving healthily is kept as such. Stagnation is the source of the malaise of the end of the Bridge. Directors thrive because they are past survival.

A NEW OTHER

Humanity has always shaped its self-image vis-à-vis the 'other', in other words, that which is not I or my group. For Directors, an immediate other will be the people of our past. Our humanity in the previous paradigm. Accepting that humans need others, we use that to reference ourselves to have an 'other'. Once we progress into a new Kuhnian paradigm it will be appropriate to differentiate ourselves in relation to 'previous people'. The differences between a person of the late Bridge and the end of Absolutism may appear shocking, but we all are cut from the same meagre cloth in the eyes of Directors. Something to be examined, contrasted with, and left behind. The first Directors will have to live among them. But it is important to reference with the Director's previous 'self' and not non-Directors because non-Directors are not the other, but Directors in waiting. That does not mean we should not defend ourselves if non-Directors abhor us, but eventually we will all be Directors and the other will be the memory of something because in a new paradigm even how we reference the 'other' may evolve. New reflexes will emerge. Humanity will be reborn. This must be if it is to contend with the non-human 'other' that is coming: the advent of AI.

ETUDE 4

Culture – An Ethnography of the Future

We surpass in foreign customs those who have been practising the same things for a long time.

Kaeso (a Roman)*

Cultures are like identities in the sense that, in the Bridge, we see ourselves as 'having a culture' or as being part of one (or several). In much of the Bridge's culture, we also see something that can be defined as beyond an ephemeral patchwork of shared ideas, feelings, and symbols. We might perceive ourselves to be custodians or inheritors of a specific culture. Some of us behave as though these cultures are 'pure' things (a tendency reinforced by nationalism's compartmentalisation of culture). A culture being 'one thing', or at least it would appear to be so if judged by the way many of us behave in relation to them. People can also be proud (or ashamed) of their

* From "Roman anecdotes of Plutarch or Caecilius" in a Vatican codex discovered by H. Von Armin in 1892.

culture. Cultures and subcultures even have names: Russian culture, European culture, American culture, race-related or ethnic cultures, and other non-national cultures. Many are the product of historical processes marred with societal trauma and suffering. Others are imposed through political means and some are the expression of creative forces. But for all, ingrained within, there is the conception that there are 'other cultures', and that a culture is an independent or semi-independent notion instead of part of a broader patchwork of a single human culture. We may have a sense of ownership over something that we feel is real although it escapes consistent definition and consensus across geography and time.

There is today a crossover between identity, culture, and nationalism. While many cultures or aspects of culture are either sub- or supranational, nationalism and the Bridgeist concept of the nation-state has meant that many of our cultures and, hence, modes of thought are bound by, or at least tethered to, a sense of physical location with all the baggage that entails. Nationalism has been around since at least the French Revolution; it is part and parcel of the birth of the Bridge. It is one of the Bridge's intrinsic features and it has extended culture's ownership of our 'selves'.

People have conceptions of what a culture is and the idea of belonging to something unique and, by definition, exclusive vis-à-vis other humans because the 'other' is central to our conception of culture as a thing in and of itself. Many of us recognise the diversity of cultural modes while acknowledging that the spectrum is, in fact, not as wide as our behavioural defaults suggest. Yet, we sometimes behave as if the other is really THE other: an enemy, an existential threat. This is an ancient and inherited reflex that, when shared by two parties, becomes the default reality allowing the worlds and mindsets of the past to maintain their grip on the present and, through it, the future. It is the perpetuation of survival instincts in a changed context.

Cultures, especially national cultures, may appear, on the surface, to be markedly different from each other. They are really just a varied assortment of geographically tethered group-selves. From a parochial perspective, these clashes of culture have reinforced our sense of difference. Yet if we viewed ourselves in the third person, from outside humanity, how similar yet tragicomically unaware might we appear?

Why does culture change? Because it is not a thing in itself. It is a collage of imagined and projected worlds that interact with each other, and in their interaction, the kaleidoscope, turned by time, is ever changing. The rate of change and adoption depends on where and when they exist.

With the arrival of the Internet, culture has been given a virtual dimension. Cultures have been uploaded, which means they have been delocalised. Cultures were once somewhere physical in terms of both the people that they 'owned' and the places where the people lived. With the Internet, cultures are no longer bound by location or a people but rather exist in a virtual space for all to access, share, appropriate, or reject. By uploading we have made cultures and their various aspects available for consumption and thus absorption. Consumables that change with each interaction with humanity. The act of uploading content relegates what it was in that moment to history. We are witnessing the true beginning of cultural wars. Virtually, people can exist and be from anywhere. What we take in from the world on our screens and reflect into our physical lives is something that can no longer be controlled.

Coupled by the frequency and distance travelled by humans, all cultures are everywhere. For those who feel either robbed or under threat, surely their entire sense of history and geography is outdated.

To truly own our share of the world as Directors we must first let go of the parts we think we own and the parts that own us and deceive us about who owns who. We must start by shedding our ownership of specific cultures so that we can be part of something bigger and wider. A new group with unlimited horizons. We must move past our sense of ownership of things because it limits us. To be a Director is to be a collector; pieces of cultures across both time and space are appropriated for better use. A Director owns by virtue of their changed relationship to things that once owned them. A Director is an evolution of their previous self.

In the Bridge people may see themselves as superior because they are 'of one or another thing or place' but what that actually means is 'I am only one thing, owned and limited'. Some people call themselves nationalists when the context is 'national culture'. This means that they are bound by an inherited understanding of what culture is, how to engage with the notion, and their horizon is much shorter than the infinity they perceived at the window. They are of something that owns them. A Director is free and whole by virtue of their multifacetedness. They enjoy the ability to select, incorporate, and appropriate and are no longer bound by one thing or place.

Culture can be appropriated safely across time because notions of obsolescence can change and ideas can be plucked out of their antiquated contexts and put into something new. In so doing they will change and become reinvigorated, healthy and useful. Some ideas and cultural modes will have value and others not but, regardless, no values will ever be imposed because, other than the mechanism of Directorship, everyone will reinvent themselves from the ideas and cultures that work for them.

Directors are not here to plunder the world and its past of ideas, norms, and symbols. They don't seize. Things are given to them by individuals and groups that join them; those who once thought they 'owned' something and now realise they don't. But how can someone give what they don't own? The realisation of lack of ownership is itself the transfer. The process of letting go of a false claim is the sharing as well as the dissipation of what once was in the annals of history. A place that will be consigned to memory. A time where people were different.

Culture will evolve because appropriated cultures and their facets will change as part of being appropriated. Nothing old will be left as it once was; it will all genuinely move on by virtue of a new form. Is this good or bad? Well, when we admire a culture we tend to admire what it once was, what we hope it might become, its struggle to preserve itself or what we think it represents and not what it really is today, and that means the things we might fear missing out on are already gone, or never were and might not ever be. It is our misplaced sense of ownership or part-ownership that we need to overcome, as well as a deluded sense of ability or need to preserve and hold still something that not only moves as part of its inherent nature but has in fact already long since moved. We are desperately clinging onto shadows of symbols and fading impressions of an imagined reality.

Anyone can become a Director. There is no exclusion. There is no boundary set by race, nation, class, or other nasty exclusionary product of the previous paradigm. An individual can even become a Director without their group. They are then either a Director-in-waiting (someone waiting for their group and vis-à-vis their group is in limbo) or they join a group of Directors. All groups will be welcome.

What are we to do about monistic cultures? Or monistic aspects of cultures? Absolutist elements will lose themselves in the transfer. Monism is about single, exclusionary, majority-held values. In Directorship, anything old becomes a minority value because there is no majority in something so vast for something that once was a majority in something smaller. In Directorship, everyone will be a minority on something that matters to them providing a genuine self-serving reason to respect others.

To become a Director we will have to leave our pasts at the door and step into a new world as an act of choice. In this new state, we will start to select and appropriate anew. We will start with nothing but the self (which is so much more than it was in the Bridge) and, devoid of our previous existence, we will become discerning collectors and worthy Directors.

But what about the past? What about history and shared suffering and trauma that can neither be denied nor forgotten? We will have to learn to let go because it is the victims and their descendants who continue to suffer and we deserve better. Perhaps the only way it can happen is if we watch the descendants of those who oppressed us, along with enough of those who still hold their views today, change with us as we all enter a new Kuhnian paradigm of genuine equality. We should have the courage to tread the same path together.

There will be questions and quarrels over ownership with non-Directors. There will be questions of transformation and authenticity. One should hear them out and wait with patience and kindness. We must outgrow our current selves and surmount our sense of self to become whole. In so doing we will add new meaning to the phrase 'get over yourself'.

Ethnographers often tell us that culture requires a shared language. The culture of Directorship will share a language in the sense that we will frame the world through the same words irrespective of the natural languages that we may speak. We will understand each other because translating what 'is' will make it so. We won't need to all speak English, French, German, or Chinese to understand. We will have something greater than a specific language; our own words for things that we can now see. A culture of freedom and tolerance where all other parts are both personal and appropriated. Where each authentic self is as a beautiful kaleidoscope seen through the tube that is Directorship.

ETUDE 5

Closing Remarks

ASPECTS OF ORGANISATION

The first Directors will live amongst the remnants of the Bridge. Its organisational structures will still stand. Nation-states may still be the default grouping and inequality of Representation (R) will be recently solved or in the process of healing. There will be backlash. Looking forward, there may be aspects of the old Organisation (O) that we choose to keep while changing some and discarding others. The process of how this is done is key to how the world transitions into structures that increase R and evolve healthily and dynamically as we grow and as our needs change. Reducing intergroup friction is also key. Systems must be developed that will enable Directors to make and implement the decisions and solutions they choose to apply to problems. The people as government. Not 'government of the people, by the people, for the people'.* We will all be proverbial founding fathers with constitutions that are born anew with each change we enact.

---

* Abraham Lincoln, *The Gettysburg Address*, 1863

The future of R in Directorship is clear but the direction of O is not. The technologies we select over time to vote and express our R may change, but the concept is static. On the other hand, O is something that cannot have an ideal structure that lasts 'forever' (the length of a paradigm), but is rather a product of needs, and needs change. The key to developing new modes of O is collaboration and experimentation. Having changed R, Directors may also decide to let O change organically. That is either prudent or stupid and there is no telling. Either way, O needs to be contemplated. The imposition of a fixed and permanent O is unwelcome. But I dare to suggest a list of topics that could be expanded and followed up on.

Entering into a new paradigm presents us with many unknown factors that are unimaginable before the start. This does not mean that we are to baulk at the scale of potential change, but rather that our Copernican moment also has the humility to say 'I don't know', and we are aware that the new paradigm forces new questions, even if it cannot answer all of them. The whole point of a new paradigm is that we can grow within it and from there move forwards. It is not a solution but a framework within which we solve and progress. Despite that, there are topics and questions that we need to be mindful of as we start; many others will rear their heads later and some may even disappear, solved by the change of paradigm. The two we will look at here are core questions. The first is grouping and the second is the structure and mechanisms of direct democracy.

In the beginning, there is the individual. Then there is grouping. It is the pre-condition for the political. Stripped bare, the interactions of individuals in groups and between groups is the political devoid of paradigm. In the context of the rare paradigmatic opportunity afforded to us by reshaping R, there are aspects of grouping that require re-examining through a new lens. Some may appear unnecessary, others urgent. Viewpoints will depend on who is asked and when. It is important to consider how groups have formed politically over the course of the first Representational Paradigm (RP). There are both voluntary and involuntary groupings. One could choose to be a 'socialist' or 'capitalist' in the late Bridge. Involuntary groupings have two subsections. First are those of circumstance, such as being born into a group attached to a certain identity, for example, 'Russian' or 'American'. Second, there are imposed involuntary groupings. For example, the nation-states of West Africa and their borders (created by colonialism), invasions, and annexations of territory, or the imposition of ideology on nations by rulers and political parties. We may want to look at what constitutes a legitimate way to form a group, or we could have no presumption of fixed groups; the fixed group is the Directors and all else is personal and ever-shifting. The end of homogeneous groups and lessening friction at the same time are a challenge we must face.

The Directors are the group, but there will naturally be subgroups, whether geographical or other. What is good for one place may not be as good for another at the same time. The role of subgroups will be to determine the future of Directorship and challenge its foundations if their relationship to voting is built wrong. There will be a transition phase from the beginning of Directorship to its more mature state. Subgroups are excluded by nature of being a subset, but not recognising diversity is equally exclusionary. Here we face several dilemmas. A majority in a subgroup will be a minority within the broader context of Directors as a group.

Everyone will learn quickly what it is like to be a minority that wants to be respected and, in turn, learn to truly respect their fellow humans.

How will a new group (Directors) organise to maximise R? What do we make of existing/old groups? Do we engage with them conceptually or have we really changed and become Directors as opposed to Bridgeist peoples with new tools of democracy? If so, then we are choosing to deliberately move on as we look to develop a planetary political culture. Globalism has hitherto failed because it came to us from the top down. It needs to be the opposite. Globalism should exist as a consequence of Directorship, neither the goal nor the cause. A new and incremental potential globalism. Breaking walls as a consequence, not a goal. A first real Organisational Paradigm (OP).

We need to focus on the primacy of the individual because that will allow the melding of groups around common issues instead of cultural association, geography, and history. That is not the way to go about putting together or organising a state in the 21st century. That was the old way.

There are also important questions around whether there is to be a system of duties. If so, what will they be? We have taken our R to use it. What do Directors vote on other than legislation, if anything?

Why is it that it takes 50% to do or undo something? Or even 50% of voters who actually voted? These percentages have little grounding other than tradition and history. Why is it not more, or less, or maybe it should depend on what is being done, or even other factors? There are so many things we have accepted that seem natural and intuitive just because we are born into a time where they are a norm. They might not mean much in a new context.

Will someone offer us DaaS – Democracy as a Service? Who will own it, or will we jointly own it, or will it belong to no one and be built collaboratively and open-source? What will it mean for R and O to have such products on offer? Who will be the customer, group, or individual? Will it be shaped like a service today? We may even choose to gamify our politics. We could set medium-term goals and, exactly like a game, create software to make a game of it for us with all the corresponding motivations, rewards, engagement, and even punishments. It wouldn't be hard to build and it could be voted in. We could be paid to do the things we decided we need to do while having fun.

After Copernicus and Galileo broke the mould, it took time for everyone to agree on a language of mathematics and physics. Once this was done, things sped up. We need a new language for a new understanding. Words, symbols, their meaning, and use. The symbols +, -, and = are less than 500 years old, but having them made sure certain things made sense to everyone.

There are many experiments to make for O. There are so many potential new worlds to explore. We need to engage with each other, collaborate, and experiment. This is how we should deal with most questions of O. It may be decided that this chapter asks all the wrong questions, in which case the new paradigm looks even more different than how I imagined it. What is imperative is that we need to make the shift. People need to start experimenting with themselves first and then in groups. Groups of equal R. Groups of Directors, who work together to perfect our means and tools to improve our world.

OTHER FACETS

There are many things that I have not mentioned. Things that have been touched by this book yet not dealt with directly. Attempting to cover everything runs the risk of not focusing on what first needs to be addressed. I have written about the issues I feel are most pressing. Our R and ourselves. There is much more to consider through the lens of Directorship. A few of these facets could not be completely left untouched, but are not core here. These are some of the things I have not spoken of yet cannot fully ignore.

OF ECONOMICS

I have not said much about economics. Economics is a product of the Bridge as are economic readings of history. A good measure of Temporal Relativism (TR) is perhaps in order here too. 'Modern' economics lies in the realm of things whose negative effects we seek to heal ourselves from. The questions of property and value, among other things, will remain with us well into the second RP.

OF ECONOMIC DISCONTENT

I will not speak of what my heart does not understand from experience. There are many things I have seen and felt for others but not endured myself. I cannot wear a mask and pose. There is anger, and Directors are beyond anger because they are in power. May Directors find in the paradigm the mechanisms and tools to find economic contentment.

OF HATE

It is only with the equality of Directorship, the true equality of shared legislative power, that we can begin to let go of intergroup hate. Only then can we embrace one another for we will be the same on the angle that unites us, allowing us all to be unique and different, yet accepted. We should not enter the new paradigm with anger, lest it consumes us and taints the second age of humankind.

OF MORALITY

Morality may change its meaning with the paradigm. It has always shifted and evolved, but its meaning has not fundamentally changed. 'Offences of R' may be a thing in the beginning. We may always have right and wrong, but the meaning of morality in the political might change. Don't let that scare you, or even excite you if you are an immoralist today. The word will have new meaning because the people uttering it will be different to those who once were.

A WORD FOR CONTEMPORARY READERS

I fear that I am 20 years too late, or too early for the true distortions of R to make people see the need. I fear that I am Sarah Connor but that my Terminator is just a set of deaf ears. That the children of Netflix, Snapchat, TikTok, and Fortnite are too busy to listen as corporations, states, and dictators with too much R take what little we have gained since 1789. There are alternatives to Directorship. Dystopias that do not look like the Bridge. They too would be the product of technology. To reach a point where we are so busy that R is lost to the fewest of the few. Drugged by our screens, AI will either be their tool to manage us or it will take the R from them. We might yet be sorry for our screen time.

GOALS: PERMANENT AND TEMPORARY

Directorship aspires to make us more cohesive in our approach to group goals. Not in the sense that we should all agree on what the problems are and what to do about them, but that we approach problems in a new way. This is not to be understood in the sense that we are all to suddenly turn into productivity freaks or start-up CEOs, but rather that a set of concepts are kept in mind when Directors are legislating. The first is conceptual yet may yield tangible results if the idea is developed further. We need to imagine our new and ever-improving 'human average'. What these attributes or their relative importance are may vary across the generations as we grow into our new selves.

TEMPORARY GOALS AND METRICS

Many societies today seem to lack goals. Of course, we are not assuming that groups should necessarily be 'cohesive' in the Bridgeist sense of the term, but rather observing a complete lack of direction. Circular movement rather than progress. Treading water only to be hit by waves. Subgoals are temporary things societies think about as they legislate towards a new human average in tangible terms. Many problems have answers in science, others in areas where a measure of TR could be of value. Nevertheless, groups must agree at least on how they measure success. GDP, GDP/capita, and other metrics are old ideas. That doesn't mean they are useless or expired. On the contrary, today they are very useful in the economic sense, but we must keep in mind that as we progress as a species we need to be open to having the types of metrics that evolve and allow for new goals to become prioritised and, at least, equally valued.

Some societies today don't actually set their goals and yet claim to be cohesive 'units' or 'nations'. This is not to suggest that we should all become obsessed with Bhutan's Happiness Index but to merely highlight the fact that there is no conscious and widespread public debate about the selection and prioritisation of metrics and issues on a strategic level. No concerted plan or lively debate around metrics, and yet we elect people to spend our money while pretending to work for us to get 'results'.

PERMANENT GOALS: MEANS NOT ENDS

One of the great dangers of Directorship is that it could be used to pursue Absolutist ends. That a person or group with a vision of a fixed world and end may try to hijack things. We are increasingly above that and the curve we will ride on with Directorship may erase these fears, but for the moment they exist. They are very real in the Bridge. What we need to do is to preserve Directorship as a mechanism, as a means. Not as an end. The vessel through which we exercise our legislative and other rights is what we need to protect. It may evolve as we move further into the paradigm, but it must not be disfigured, no matter how attractive a would-be representative makes that change look in a time of crisis. Our goal is to establish, build, use, maintain, and protect a means. A tool for freedom, equality, and prosperity.

A means to change the meaning of politics and catapult ourselves into progress.

Politics is the cornerstone of social science. In the same way that physics affects chemistry, biology, botany, and gardening in turn, if we change the political and move that proverbial cornerstone, all else will fall into place behind it. The new RP can change the meaning of so many things, erase old problems, and allow us to fix those that arise. Many areas of human experience have progressed. It is that which has progressed the least that must have its watershed moment. That we may all become a Copernicus together by way of Directorship.

THE LAST

We only need to change one aspect of politics to change everything: the value of R. A letter imbibed with the heavy meaning of inequality and our relationship to it must change forever. There are things, of course, that we must change in ourselves, but the inequalities of R are what we all suffer in common. The generation that starts this process will be the last to have lived in the first RP and the last to be oppressed in this specific way. They will be the last, and in a sense, they will also be the first. The first to be truly free. The first legitimate lawmakers. The first human gods to democratise the tools of creation. Re-reading the Bridge's political thought and history through the lens of Directorship makes us realise that we only need to change one thing for everything to change and for a broken paradigm to be shed.

Directorship can shift us to a world where the meaning of politics is made anew. A paradigm where there is natural development of a nuanced view of issues and of the transitory and only partial value of facets of the old Bridgeist Political Beliefs. A world where we become who we are: a single pantheon where everyone is a part-time legislator. We have been conditioned to be slaves for so long and it has worked because freedom and the worth of a person have been defined for us. It is time for each of us to define them permanently.

We do not seek a utopia or the u-human but rather to see what we are not so that we may imagine what we can be, making it possible if only we dare to take what we have denied ourselves. If equality of R were a metric of human development, we would observe ourselves the way a person of the late Bridge sees a tribe of jungle-dwelling cannibals. Utterly primitive and in no way quaint. We have succeeded on so many of the metrics of the Bridge and its 'prosperity metrics'. It is time to choose goals where we are still low on the uphill road. We must evolve or fall. Will we do it? That may depend on 'will' itself. We don't have to behave like we are from the Bridge. That is the first step to becoming a Director.

PEOPLE 'OF BRIDGEIST DEMOCRACIES'

You have the tools built into the system to replace it. This means that the mechanisms for the legitimisation of RP2 in the eyes of the Bridge are pre-existing. Through temporary representatives, elections can be won fair and square by Bridgeist rules. This is just a means to a new means. It can be forgiven on the grounds that it is a transition phase but beware of those who would use it to maintain the status quo. If representative democracy is to do the world a final favour it is that, in some places, the best of the old paradigm paved the way for its end. How will we know when a representative democracy is ready? When it votes itself peacefully into becoming something new and legitimises the rebirth of politics.

PEOPLE 'OF DICTATORSHIPS'

I lived for most of my life under a dictatorship. I went through phases of both blind adoration and intense hatred for it and its symbols. Now I am beyond these emotions because I am the First of the Last. I look back at them through the eyes of a new paradigm. 'I am the First of the Last.' Say it out loud and smile. We have honour that can't be understood by those who came before and that will never be forgotten by those who come after. The extension of the evolution inside of us will flow to many and will become a physical reality in the world of R and O. This is a matter of time and persistence.

The products of dictatorship speak for themselves and they lead to revolt. It is here that the injustices of R are most pronounced. We find it in the sufferings of many at the hands of a few and sometimes the other few who revolt to 'emancipate' the many.

There is, for those who live in a dictatorship, only one way forward. The event of a real referendum. A direct vote on the immediate application of Directorship. It must be voted in and this is crucial. The replacement of representatives without incremental milestones. The ugly and expired mirage of representative democracy as the next step for dictatorships is like a shiny yet slippery pebble. Dull and fragile when placed next to a diamond, it can hold no human weight for long. It is not a stepping stone, just a less acute, Western strain of the same illness. Diagnosed by a lack of R.

How does one force a referendum? There are two safe ways and one dangerous way. The safe ways are: 1. Peaceful critical mass which leads to a vote; 2. A king or dictator sees the end of the paradigm, and in his quest for a legacy sees something more permanent than what he seeks for his regime. An immortal personal legacy worthy of an Alexander or a Caesar. He ushers in the referendum because he can. Poetic and immortal he surrenders his R to others for its dissemination. There is no halfway.

The third way is the dangerous and undesirable way. A small group (rebels or revolutionaries) choose to represent (or even just start to push) and take over to 'liberate', 'allow', or 'facilitate' people to vote. This is either greed or ism in disguise. It is the old paradigm trying to mirror something vital and wear a new mask to save itself. Even an ailing paradigm may fight to survive and it knows the old ways work. So far, they always have. There is no place for either this or violence in Directorship.

If people have become dangerous as Aristotle's political animals (beings that group), it is because the politics of our context has kept us as animals. To become our true selves we must first take our freedom from those who hold the keys. One could ask, 'are we doomed not to see the arrival of a new paradigm because there is no ideal route to it?' On the contrary, if we change ourselves, the paradigm will begin and it will appear organically. The question is: can we all evolve our 'self' at sufficient speed to survive and outgrow our current predicament and save our species, our environment, and be truly different when the real 'other' of AI becomes what it will be?

OF SOUNDS

What does the arrival of Directorship sound like? It is a highly personal question worth pondering. Listen for it and don't think. The music that heralds Directorship will be different to each of us. Most importantly, if you hear the beating of war drums then you are either a representative or have embraced the mechanism without the tenets that shape a true Director. All other sounds born of kindness, beauty, and hope are acceptable. If you can't shed the Bridge then throw this book away and forget you read it. For me, it's the first movement of Mendelssohn's *Violin Concerto in E minor, Op. 64*. The two currents of the individual violin and the massive orchestra interacting harmoniously, and yet it is the individual violin that that 'takes' the lead. It is not introduced or overwhelmed by the orchestra like in many concertos that came before. The orchestra exists to give expression to the individual violin. They are in harmony. Neither impedes the other.

SOME MORE THOUGHTS

There have been few contemporary political examples and case studies in this book. This is for two reasons. First, I do not know when you will read the book. Second, whether it resonates or not will depend on your own experiences; that is, on your contemporary context. If it does not resonate then I hope it is because you are freer than people were in the first decades of the millennium and that your prospects are better and not that you have passed into a post-Bridgeist dystopia of lower R.

Directorship presupposes equality of R as its foundation. From that, all other equalities stem. This does not mean that they will happen automatically but rather that equalities will change over time and that people in the new paradigm will have their own priorities. We must look forward to the day when many of the Bridge's other inequalities die out.

Without the changes we need to make in ourselves before and as we become Directors, we will never truly be free, even if we were to wrap ourselves in the trappings of a hollow Directorship. It is but a vehicle, and where we take it will make its meaning.

Absolutism and the Bridge phases are the political expressions of a wider, Western, and in some ways global, war. The Great War of the Bridge. That of monism and relativism. It started before the Bridge and it is most pronounced today. We must draw from both to kill them and in the process heal.

Apathy is the natural state of those who decide nominally, suffer directly, and can blame elected officials and themselves only through their election of the official, not for the consequence of specific decisions. Directorship will ensure that people consciously own issues. Do not fear apathy, it will die with the old paradigm.

If you think it cannot be done then you are a creature born of paternalism. Either you represent it or you have succumbed to its modes of thinking. Either way, you are its victim.

Without TR, Directorship could be used as a conduit for an ism to become an OP. This would be the greatest betrayal of

Directorship, to use its forms but not its tenets for Bridgeist or even Absolutist ends.

Let us not forget that tomorrow begins today. If you are one of those who says we are not ready, you are either afraid or suffer from a disproportionally high level of R and you see yourself as losing.

The First of the Last

We are the last
Breaking with our past
That we may see
What it is to be free

The last of the oppressed
The last of the dispossessed
The last of the forgotten
In a world turned rotten

Before the Bridge they owned us
But now the system does
Under the bus it has thrown us
Built for them it was
Those folks who say 'I represent'

There's a paradigm to break
Old selves to shake
Everything is at stake
The rest they want to take

We are the First of the Last
Breaking with our past
From the time of oppression
Of total dispossession
Let no one be forgotten
Healing a world turned rotten

We see this world lucidly
Us of the periphery
Together, individually
We build what can be

That our children may live
In a world we want to give
To them to inherit
Systems based on merit

We are the First of the Last
And to the world we say:

Hold up your pens
Those hammers
Raise them high
And strike your vote

They think we'll just break
But break free we will
To build, like they never could

And if you live
In a place that does not give
A shit about voting
Where tyrants hold you choking

Dictators of today
Living in yesterday
It's the end of the Bridge
Oppressors stand on cliff's ridge

No pens to vote?
On your voice rely
Keep your pen for voting pure
Once your Directorship is secure

Hold up your hammers
Pens to heal
Make our new paradigm real.

Glossary of Terms

Absolutism	See Absolutist Phase.
Absolutist Phase	The first of two phases of the first Representational Paradigm (RP1). This can be loosely described as starting in antiquity and ending with the French Revolution.
Ascription	The act of choosing to place belief in an idea or conceptual notion as a leap of faith within a specific theoretical framework.
Axis of Ancients	A triumvirate of three ancient thinkers: Galen, Ptolemy, and Aristotle.
BPB	Bridgeist Political Belief. This encompasses all our modern political beliefs and affiliated notions.
DaaS	Democracy as a Service.
Director	A person whose R=1.
Director-in-waiting	A person who wishes to see the implementation of Directorship but whose group has yet to align with their views.
Directorship	The name of the second Representational Paradigm (RP2) argued for in this book.

Eitopia	The potential world. A positive vision of life on Earth in contrast to Ontopia.
Florentine Prince	Machiavelli's work, *The Prince* (1513).
Ontopia	The place that is. Signifying the world we live in today, in its current state.
Re-claiming	The conceptual notion of a collective engagement to allocate certain activities as being 'purely human' and the prohibition of Artificial Intelligence from playing a role.
Representational Paradigm	A Kuhnian paradigm in politics which is defined by the mode of political representation of a given time period.
RP1	The first Representational Paradigm. We are currently in RP1.
RP2	A second, theoretical Representational Paradigm. This could or would emerge under different guises. e.g. R=1 or R=0.
Temporal Relativism	An approach to BPBs. Please see Etude 1.
The Bridge	The second phase of the first Representational Paradigm in which we exist today.
Topia	Ancient Greek word for 'Place'.

Select Bibliography

Aristotle. *The Politics and the Constitution of Athens*. Edited by Stephen Everson. United Kingdom: Cambridge University Press, 1996.

Arvon, Henri. *La Philosophie Du Travail*. France: Presses Universitaires de France, 1960.

Berlin, Isaiah. *The Hedgehog and the Fox*. United Kingdom: Phoenix, 1999.

Boyer, Carl B. and Uta C. Merzbach *A History of Mathematics*. Ukraine: Wiley, 2011.

Braghramian, Maria. "A Brief History of Relativism", in *Relativism: A Contemporary Anthology*. Edited by Michael Krausz. United States: Columbia University Press, 2010.

Buber, Martin. *I and Thou*. United Kingdom: Bloomsbury Academic, 2013.

Cairns, Huntington. *Legal Philosophy from Plato to Hegel*. United States: University of Minnesota Press, 1980.

Carey, John (ed.). *The Faber Book of Utopias*. United Kingdom: Faber and Faber, 1999.

Cicero, Marcus Tullius. *On Duties*. Edited by M. T. Griffin and E. M. Atkins. United Kingdom: Cambridge University Press, 1991.

Copernicus, Nicolaus. *Copernicus: On the Revolutions of the Heavenly Spheres*. United States: Prometheus Books, 1995.

Declaration of the Rights of Man (1789) https://avalon.law.yale.edu/18th_century/rightsof.asp

Dworkin, Ronald. *Law's Empire (Legal Theory)*. United Kingdom: Hart, 2003.

Dyson, Freeman J. *The Scientist as Rebel*. United Kingdom: New York Review Books, 2006.

Feuerbach, Ludwig. *The Essence of Religion*. United States: Prometheus Books, 2004.

Feyerabend, Paul. *Against Method*. United Kingdom: Verso, 2010.

Friedmann, Wolfgang. *Legal Theory*. United Kingdom: Stevens and Sons, 1944.

Grayling, A. C. *Wittgenstein*. United Kingdom: Oxford University Press, 1988.

Hartog, François. *Le Miroir D'Hérodote: Essai Sur la Représentation de L'Autre*. France: Gallimard, 2001.

Hobbes, Thomas. *Leviathan*. United Kingdom: Atria Books, 2008.

Horwich, Paul (ed.). *World Changes: Thomas Kuhn and the Nature of Science*. United States: The MIT Press, 1993.

Izenberg, Gerald. *Identity. The Necessity of a Modern Idea*. United States: University of Pennsylvania Press, 2016.

Kuhn, Thomas, S. *The Copernican Revolution: Planetary Astronomy in the Development of Western Thought*. United States: Harvard University Press, 2003.

Kuhn, Thomas S. and Ian Hacking. *The Structure of Scientific Revolutions* (50th Anniversary ed). United States: University of Chicago Press, 2012.

Lifton, Robert Jay. *The Protean Self: Human Resilience in an Age of Fragmentation*. United States: Basic Books, 1993.

Lincoln, Abraham. *The Gettysburg Address* (19 November 1863). http://www.abrahamlincolnonline.org/lincoln/speeches/gettysburg.htm

Lloyd, Dennis. *The Idea of Law*. United Kingdom: Abe Books, 1964.

Locke, John. *Two Treatises of Government*. Edited by Peter Laslett. Russia: Cambridge University Press, 1988.

Machiavelli, Niccolò. *The Prince*. Edited by Quentin Skinner and Russell Price (2nd ed.). United Kingdom: Cambridge University Press, 2019.

Mill, John Stuart. *On Socialism*. United States: Prometheus Press, 1987.

Montaigne, Michel de. *Die Essais*. Germany: Gallimard 1962.

Montesquieu. *De l'Esprit des Lois*. Edited by Laurent Versini. France: Gallimard, 1748; reprinted 1995.

Nagel, Thomas. "Value: Realism and Objectivity", in *Relativism: A Contemporary Anthology*. Edited by Michael Krausz. United States: Columbia University Press, 2010.

Nietzsche, Friedrich. *Beyond Good and Evil*. United Kingdom: Cambridge University Press, 2002.

Nietzsche, Friedrich. *The Gay Science*. United Kingdom: Cambridge University Press, 2001.

Nietzsche, Friedrich. *Nietzsche: On the Genealogy of Morality and Other Writings*. United Kingdom: Cambridge University Press, 2017.

Nietzsche, Friedrich. *Nietzsche: Thus Spoke Zarathustra*. Edited by Robert Pippin, translated by Adrian Del Caro. United Kingdom: Cambridge University Press, 2011.

Plato. *The Republic*. United Kingdom: Cambridge University Press, 2000.

Pomper, Philip. *The Structure of Mind in History*. United States: Columbia University Press, 1985.

Pope Leo XIII Rerum Novarum. *On Capital and Labour*. United Kingdom: St Athanasius Press, 2016.

Rawls, John. *A Theory of Justice*. India: Harvard University Press, 2005.

Ridley, Aaron (ed.). *Nietzsche: The Anti-Christ, Ecce Homo, Twilight of the Idols: And Other Writings*. United Kingdom: Cambridge University Press, 2005.

Schiller, Friedrich. *The Poems of Schiller*. Edited by Ann C. Weaver, Martin Swales, and Matthew Bell. United Kingdom: G. Bell and Sons, 1893.

Siedentop, Larry. *Inventing the Individual: The Origins of Western Liberalism*. United Kingdom: Penguin Books, 2014.

Sigmund, Paul E. (ed.). *St. Thomas Aquinas on Politics and Ethics: A New Translation, Backgrounds, Interpretations*. Norton Critical Edition. United States: W. W. Norton, 1988.

Strong, Tracy B. *Friedrich Nietzsche and the Politics of Transfiguration*. United States: University of California Press, 1988.

Sproat, Ian (ed.). *The Complete Works of Alexander Pushkin*. 9:201–232. United Kingdom: Milner and Co., 2000.

Thucydides: *The War of the Peloponnesians and the Athenians*. United States: Cambridge University Press, 2013.

The U.S. Constitution. https://constitution.congress.gov/constitution/

Waldron, Jeremy. *The Dignity of Legislation*. United Kingdom: Cambridge University Press, 1999.

Waldron, Jeremy. *One Another's Equals: The Basis of Human Equality*. United Kingdom: Harvard University Press, 2017.

Waldron, Jeremy, Wai-chee Dimock, Don Herzog, and Michael Rosen. *Dignity, Rank, and Rights*. United Kingdom: Oxford University Press, 2015.

Wittgenstein, Ludwig. *Philosophical Investigations*. Translated by P. M. S. Hacker, G. E. M. Anscombe, and Joachim Schulte. United Kingdom: Wiley, 2009.

Wootton, David. *The Invention of Science: A New History of the Scientific Revolution*. United Kingdom: Penguin Books, 2016.

Zweig, Stefan. *Montaigne*. Germany: Steerforth Press, 2015.